DUKE:
A Love Story

'A stunning, deeply moving book'
Theatreprint

'A book that will move many readers ... The John Wayne who emerges in the book is not the tough, laconic cowboy of the screen, but a tender, loving, generous and humorous man'
Irish Independent

'Pat has written of those years sensitively, with class and dignity and warmth'
Maureen O'Hara

'This is the off-stage intimacy to match the on-screen legend'
Birmingham Sunday Mercury

'She has written a warm, honest account of her seven years with the top box-office star of all time. She vividly portrays his stubborn, impulsive character and kind heart ... written with dignity, sensitive to the feelings of others and the worldwide affection for John Wayne'
Torquay Herald Express

DUKE:
A Love Story

An Intimate Memoir of
John Wayne's Last Years

Pat Stacy
with Beverly Linet

CORGI BOOKS

DUKE: A Love Story

A CORGI BOOK 0 552 12539 3

Originally published in Great Britain by Souvenir Press Ltd.

PRINTING HISTORY

Souvenir Press edition published 1983
Corgi edition published 1985

This book is set in 10/11 Baskerville

Corgi Books are published by Transworld Publishers Ltd.,
Century House, 61-63 Uxbridge Road, Ealing, London W5 5SA

Made and printed in Great Britain by
Hunt Barnard Printing Ltd., Aylesbury, Bucks.

For ED O'ROURKE,
who sold me on "getting on with it" and directed the way

ACKNOWLEDGMENTS

For their support and input, sincere thanks to my dear friends who were still there when I needed them: Claire Trevor Bren, Maureen O'Hara, Joe and Barbara DeFranco, Ken and Glenia Reafsnyder, Jack and Ruth Gordean, and Francis J. Sorg, Jr.

A special thank-you to Pilar Wayne, Aissa, and Marisa for including me in their life "after Duke."

My deep appreciation to Katharine Hepburn and Barbara Walters for allowing the use of their material. They were always, along with Lauren Bacall, "as close as the nearest telephone" during those trying times of the "life watch."

I am particularly indebted to all of Duke's doctors, who made it possible for Duke to "stay around a whole lot longer"; especially to Dr. Roman DeSanctis of Massachusetts General Hospital in Boston, and to Duke's devoted nurse, Alice Day, of UCLA Medical Center in Los Angeles.

For his assistance with medical terms, our thanks to Dr. Donald Rubell of Beth Israel and Lenox Hill Hospitals, New York City.

To Elaine Porchetti, Duke's greatest fan, who continued her everlasting devotion by sending me tapes of Duke's voice, which evoked so many vivid memories of the public appearances I shared with him.

To George L. Skypeck, "Sky," for his time and energy in supplying the behind-the-scenes story of Duke's trip to Harvard.

And to my editor, Neil Nyren—thank you for being a *real* person and a gentleman of impeccable taste.

To my dear friends Peggy Reagan and Joanne Reeves, who were and are always there when I need someone to talk to.

And to *all* of my family—thank you for your patience with me during some trying times while this memoir was being written. I know I wasn't the ideal person to be around and to live with. My sincere appreciation for your support and enthusiasm . . . and for believing in me.

PREFACE

June 11, 1983, will mark the fourth anniversary of Duke's death. As I have every year, I will go to Pacific View Memorial Park and lay a spray of anthuriums by his graveside.

Shortly after Duke died, a friend told me Duke had said to him, "Pat's still a young woman. I want her to go on and have a happy life when I'm gone. But I sure hope she doesn't forget old Duke."

Forget ? How could one forget John Wayne ?

Maureen O'Hara described him as "gruff as a bear, soft as a marshmallow, steady and reliable as a rock." Louise Brooks, upon first meeting him, thought, "This is no actor but the hero of all mythology miraculously brought to life." And Katharine Hepburn, asked to sum him up very late in his life, said simply, "He's gentle. He's a monster. He's a man."

Duke was all that, and more. I know. Duke and I were together for nearly seven years. During all those years I was his secretary and companion; for the last five, the only woman he loved.

Because of Duke, I knew the best of times and the worst of times. I was the recipient of his overwhelming generosity and love and, toward the end of his life, his understandable rage and frustrations as well. With Duke I met presidents and royalty, and traveled the world over. By his side I attended the greatest of banquets and the most intimate gatherings of his friends. And when at last, grievously, the vigil ended, I was by his bedside to mourn.

A few months ago I returned to Newport Beach to

lunch with Pilar Wayne, Duke's last wife, and her daughters by Duke, Aissa and Marisa. We wanted to reminisce about the man we had loved, each in her own way. As I was driving along the freeway, my attention was diverted by a billboard advertising the Movieland Wax Museum. At its center was a gigantic image of Duke and the words HOW TALL DID JOHN WAYNE STAND?

I have no need to see Duke lifelessly re-created in wax. No reproduction can answer that question. Perhaps in some way this book will.

Among his treasures Duke kept a small, gold-plated plaque with the saying A KIND WORD. That was his favorite motto. I'd ask if he wanted a cold drink or a cup of coffee, or perhaps a sandwich, and he'd always reply, "Yes, and a kind word." Always—"a kind word."

Duke had another favorite line, which came from his movie *The Man Who Shot Liberty Valance*. The character portrayed by Jimmy Stewart has finished his tale, revealing the truth about the shooting, and a young reporter is asked whether he plans to use the story. His answer is no. "When the legend becomes fact, print the legend." Whenever Duke was annoyed by a story about him, he'd just shrug and say, "What the hell—when the legend becomes fact, print the legend."

But I'm not writing about the legend. Too many already have, and it has become carved into the American consciousness, as if he were another granite face peering down from Mount Rushmore. That wasn't Duke.

My story is about the man I knew for seven years. And it is written with love—and a kind word.

PAT STACY
Marina Del Rey, California
December, 1982

PROLOGUE

I listened to the theme from *The High and the Mighty* reverberate throughout the Dorothy Chandler Pavilion, and then there was Duke, standing tall atop the winding staircase that led to the stage.

The audience erupted into applause as he descended and took his place before the microphones. Exactly a year before, Duke had been in Massachusetts General Hospital undergoing heart surgery, and Bob Hope had stopped the show with the wish that Duke could 'amble out here in person next year.' Now Duke smiled gratefully and allowed the applause to abate before beginning the brief speech he had lovingly prepared and memorized.

'That's about the only medicine a fella'd ever really need. Believe me when I tell you I'm mighty pleased that I can *amble* down here tonight. Oscar and I have something in common. Oscar first came to the Hollywood scene in 1928. So did I. We're both a little weather-beaten, but we're still here and plan to be around a whole lot longer.' He then went on to announce the year's Best Picture winner. It was a picture he had not cared for, *The Deer Hunter,* but his disappointment over the Academy's selection was diminished by his elation at the reception he had received from his peers—and by the fact that he had been able to get through the ceremony at all.

Everyone at the auditorium and millions of people around the world on April 9, 1979, were aware that Duke had undergone a nine-hour operation for stomach cancer just three months earlier. Although he was painfully thin, many believed that he had beaten 'the Big C' yet again, just as he had fifteen years earlier when he had had a cancerous lung removed.

No one—except Duke; his thirteen-year-old daughter, Marisa; and me—knew what it had taken for him to get out on that stage that night. It had been a rough day.

Early that morning Duke had gone to Hoag Hospital, in Newport Beach, for his daily radiation treatment, which was always an ordeal; then he had had to endure the hour-and-a-half drive to Los Angeles for the dress rehearsal. We went in his motor home, which Duke usually used as a dressing room when he worked on location and which contained a bed, enabling him to rest until we arrived at the Los Angeles Music Center. Although the Monday dress rehearsal usually proceeded in the same order as the final telecast, we were told they'd run through Duke's segment as soon as he arrived; there'd be no tedious waiting around. The show's producer even wanted to eliminate the staircase from the rehearsal, but Duke said, 'I might as well see if I can handle it now, and not make a damn fool of myself during the show.' He refused to be treated as an invalid.

He allowed himself a few concessions, however. He sensibly decided to forgo sitting through the entire show, and regretfully turned down the invitation to the governors' ball that followed. 'That would be stretching it,' he said. He had wanted badly to go to the ball—had wanted Marisa and me to have a wonderful time—but he couldn't dance, couldn't eat, couldn't have as much as a single drink. The frustration would have been terrible.

Duke had reserved accommodations at the Bonaventure Hotel, a few minutes from the auditorium, in order to have a place where he could nap after the rehearsals and where we could dress before the show. Although Marisa and I were to remain back stage with Duke, he had insisted on our buying new dresses for the event.

'But, Duke,' I had said, 'I have a dozen party dresses. And no one will even notice us.'

'I'll see you,' he had replied. 'And, besides, I want Marisa to *feel* special. She was only three and couldn't come along the night I won for *True Grit,* and I promised her to take her to one of these things when she was older. Bad enough it has to be this way, but who knows when I'll be able to take her again. I want her to look like a princess.'

The Oscar telecast started at seven P.M. California time. Our plan was to dine in our room and watch the show until it was time for us to leave. Duke hadn't eaten all day; he barely touched the soft food we had ordered for him.

Dave Grayson, Duke's longtime makeup man, arrived at the hotel shortly before eight to prepare him for the cameras. Acutely aware of his gauntness, Duke instructed Dave, 'Go easy. I'd rather not look as if I'd just been embalmed.'

I no longer had any doubts about Duke's getting through the evening. I knew he would. As long as he could walk and use his voice, he was determined to turn his appearance into a personal triumph. Nevertheless, as we raced to the theater, I couldn't help worrying about him and wondering why he was pushing himself so soon after his surgery.

In retrospect, however, I believe Duke was there to bid a glorious and fond farewell—to the industry, to his friends, to the world.

It was past nine when Barney Fotheringham, Duke's driver, pulled up to the rear entrance of the Chandler Pavilion. What a sight we must have been, with Duke in his tuxedo, Marisa and me in our pretty dresses, emerging from a motor home. An official greeter awaited to usher us into a private room, so we'd not be disturbed.

We weren't alone for long, though. Word slipped out that Duke had arrived, and people started coming

15

around. No one was going to bar Lord Laurence Olivier or Cary Grant from the room. The conversation among the three great stars was just small talk. Grant and Duke mainly talked about their young daughters: Marisa had been born just four days before Jennifer Grant, in February, 1966. I remember Duke asking about Jennifer, and Grant wistfully replying that he didn't see her as often as he wished. I think he envied Duke's having Marisa with him that night.

Later, when we were alone, Marisa asked, 'Pat, who were those two old men Dad was talking to?' Marisa didn't think of Duke as an old man.

I also remember Lauren Bacall rushing in and out, demanding, 'Where's Duke? Where is he? He's the only one here I want to see'; and Jane Fonda, Duke's longtime political adversary and Best Actress winner that night for another anti-Vietnam-war film, *Coming Home*, dropping in to say a few encouraging words to her father's close friend and the man who had bounced her on his lap when she'd been a shy child.

After the presentation Duke impulsively dropped into the press room to congratulate the winners. Although he begged off on interviews, telling reporters to call him at home the next day, and declined to pose for the standard shot of presenter standing with winner, he good-naturedly obliged a photographer who asked for a couple of shots of him alone. That was a mistake.

On television Duke had looked wonderful: lithe and young. (This is not my memory playing tricks on me. The Academy graciously ran the videotape of his segment for me as I was beginning this memoir.) The still photos told another story. The look of death was etched on Duke's face, was reflected in his eyes. When I saw the pictures later, I was stunned and sickened. I suppose it is similar to looking at yourself in the mirror every day: you don't see yourself getting older. I had been with Duke constantly. Some days he looked better than others, but it was not until I saw those pictures that I became fully aware of the horrifying deterioration that had taken place over the past few months.

And then there was the pain. I knew that Duke suffered badly—how could I not?—not only from the physical pain but from the mental agony of dying and the frustration of losing control. But it was not until thirteen days later that I was to know the true extent of that suffering.

That night at the Academy Awards, Duke stayed only a few minutes in the press room; then he rejoined Marisa and me and we slipped out the back way and into the motor home, unnoticed, and were driven straight back to Newport. Marisa stayed overnight with her father; the next morning, it was radiation as usual.

Thirteen days later, in a moment of despair, Duke ordered me to get the Smith & Wesson .38 he kept beside his bed, because, he said, 'I want to blow my brains out.'

Part I
The Highs

CHAPTER 1

IT all began with a simple telephone call.

John Wayne didn't hire me as his personal secretary because he'd been dazzled by my beauty or wit, or knocked out by my secretarial skills, though the latter were pretty good. Ironically, John Wayne *never* hired me. He took me sight unseen, and I'd been on the payroll for nearly three weeks before we were even formally introduced.

Being a romantic, I'd like to think it was predestined that we would meet, connect, fall in love. However, it was only through an accident of timing that I chanced into the job that changed the course of my life.

I had been working at the accounting firm of Arthur Andersen & Co. in Los Angeles when my boss was informed he was being transferred to Chicago. He asked me if I wanted to come, too, but I loved California—had ever since I'd moved there from my native Louisiana four years before. As much as I liked my job, I liked my adopted home state more, and I was confident I could find something suitable.

Then that happy accident of timing occurred. William Neuhauser, the head of the tax division at Arthur Andersen, phoned and asked, 'Pat, how would you like to work with John Wayne?'

For a few seconds I thought he was putting me on. Work with John Wayne? Other than attending the movies regularly and cutting out Jane Powell paper dolls as a little girl, I knew nothing about Hollywood. Arthur Andersen & Co. did, however; they handled the tax affairs of dozens of movie people, including John

Wayne.

And that's what the call was all about. William Neuhauser had been acquainted with Mary St John, Wayne's executive secretary, for nearly three decades. Mary had told him she was planning to retire but didn't want to leave Wayne's employ until she had found and trained a suitable replacement. Wayne had entrusted her with that responsibility without reservation. He had that much faith in her judgement.

After I was assured that my inexperience in the industry would be more of an advantage than a detriment—Mary St John didn't want a starry-eyed fan or would-be actress on the staff—I applied for the position. The salary wasn't spectacular—two hundred dollars a week—less than some of the big industrial companies were offering for experienced secretaries at the time. But at least, I thought, it was something different. Who could have dreamed just how different.

And who knows how I might have acted had Duke conducted that initial interview himself. I may not have been a starry-eyed fan, but still—this was John Wayne. I doubt if I would have been as cool and confident as I was with Mary St John. Mary was a crisp, no-nonsense lady who knew exactly what she was looking for, and somehow I convinced her that I fit the bill.

'You've got the job,' she told me, and then went on to list the details. I'd be working out of Wayne's production company, Batjac, whose office was then located at Paramount Studios. About twice a week we'd work with Wayne at his Newport Beach home at 2686 Bayshore Drive. My primary duties, at least at the beginning, would involve taking care of his business and personal mail, answering the fan mail, and sending out autographed photos. She made it quite clear that Wayne—unlike some other major stars—insisted that the mail be answered and the photo requests honored. 'He feels,' Mary told me, 'that the fans were responsible for making him a star and keeping him a star, and

21

he's not about to ignore them now. Remember—he's *adamant* about that.'

And so in mid-June, a few weeks after my thirty-first birthday, I had myself a new job.

When I telephoned my father back in Louisiana and told him who I'd gone to work for, he didn't believe me. My whole family had been Wayne fans for a long time, and the idea of having a daughter working for him sounded like a fairy tale. 'What's he like?' my father asked.

'I have no idea,' I replied. 'I haven't met him.'

At that, my dad really thought I was kidding him. I had to explain that Wayne was in Hawaii right then, attending the wedding of his good friend Chick Iverson, and I promised to call as soon as I had met the invisible man.

I was a mass of nerves until I did. The job was simple enough, even fun. Mary St John seemed impressed with the way I learned things, but I wondered if I would live up to Wayne's standards. After all, he was used to Mary and her way of doing things. She would be a tough act to follow.

Finally the big day came: Wayne was back and I was to meet him. It was similar to a blind date, I thought: two strangers hoping that by the grace of God they'd hit it off. And we seemed to. The meeting itself was almost anticlimactic, but I recall being surprised that he was heavier than I'd expected, and that he wore a toupee. I was also delighted by his warm and un-assuming style, which put me completely at ease. I began by calling him Mr Wayne, and he put a halt to that immediately. 'The name's Duke,' he said. And 'Duke' he was from then on, in private. In public, I was still careful to call him Mr Wayne.

I wasn't keeping a scrapbook or diary at that time, though I would later; therefore, nowhere is it written, in big, bold script, TODAY I MET DUKE! How ironic that although we'd celebrate so many birthdays, holidays, and anniversaries together, neither of us could ever

22

pinpoint what I'd come to think of as 'the first day of the rest of my life.'

Duke didn't do much dictation that first day. It was more of a 'getting acquainted' kind of afternoon. I was introduced to his wife, Pilar, who was cordial and charming, a perfect hostess, and to their three children: Aissa, sixteen; John Ethan, ten; and little Marisa, a six-year-old doll. They seemed such a loving family; there was so much kissing and hugging between father and children, and I vividly remember thinking how different it was from when I was growing. My parents had frowned upon open displays of affection, and there'd been very little kissing and hugging and touching in my family.

As Mary and I drove back to Paramount that afternoon, I asked her why Duke and the family lived so far from town. Mary explained that the Waynes had owned a magnificent house in Encino, in the San Fernando Valley, for ten years, but then Duke had fallen in love with a boat: a 136-foot converted minesweeper he called the *Wild Goose*. For five years the family had divided their time between the *Goose* and movie locations, until finally, impulsively, they had put the Encino house on the market and moved into a motel apartment in Newport Beach, where the *Goose* was berthed. Newport Beach had resembled a sleepy little fishing village then, and Duke had been so attracted to it he'd bought a house and settled down there. Since then, the town had turned into a bustling business and industrial community, but the Bayshore area had remained relatively untouched by such 'progress,' and since it was in such close proximity to the *Goose*, Duke still preferred it to anything Los Angeles or Beverly Hills had to offer. After his neighbors had got used to having him in their midst, he was able to go about his business relatively undisturbed. The only people who bothered him were boaters who came too close to his private pier or to the *Goose*, hoping to catch a glimpse or a greeting.

23

Mary St John was far too discreet to discuss Duke's relationship with Pilar. I knew that they'd been married for nearly eighteen years, and that the press had described their union in glowing terms. I had no idea then, and would not learn until much later, that Duke and Pilar had been seeing family counselors in an attempt to save their marriage. Nor did I know that in 1958 Pilar had actually decided on a divorce, and that after a short separation Duke had persuaded her to change her mind. The problem was an old one for wives and husbands of stars: Pilar was working hard to establish an identity other than that of 'Mrs John Wayne.' Duke once remarked ruefully, 'Pilar felt I was trying to smother her personality.' In addition, Pilar never could get used to the constant invasion of privacy that came with being married to Duke. It was especially hard when he was off making a movie and she had to cope alone with endless intrusions from the public and the press.

I was unaware of any of this, however, during my first six months working for Duke. Pilar was always gracious to me, and often, when Duke was busy with Mary St John, Pilar would borrow me to aid her in details requiring secretarial help.

She was engrossed in starting a tennis club in Newport, for instance, and, passionately absorbed in tennis, she was always dashing off to some tournament or other. Duke himself seemed uninterested in the game. He preferred spending his leisure time at the Big Canyon Country Club, playing backgammon, chess, or liars' poker with his friends.

I worked at Newport Beach only two days a week. Duke would dictate for up to five hours; then Mary and I would return to the studio. At that time a great deal of his mail was of a political nature. He was actively campaigning for Richard Nixon's re-election, always dashing off to some rally or party.

I doubt if Duke and I were alone for more than five minutes at any given time during that period. Our relationship was all business. Or was it? Occasionally I'd mention where I'd been the night before with the man I was dating at that time and would detect a look of annoyance on Duke's face. I attributed it to the fact that he didn't care much for his employees' bringing their personal life to work with them, so I tried not to do that. My personal life was, in fact, rather chaotic. I was involved with a businessman, but we were having our share of difficulties, and, having gone through a disastrous two-year marriage before settling in California, I was gun-shy at the possibility of a binding relationship. I loved my freedom and my new job, and as the months flew by, I realized to my great distress that I was beginning to love my boss.

It was an unrequited love, I was sure, and so I did my best to hide my feelings from my friends, from Mary St John, from Pilar, but most of all from Duke. And I was successful with everyone, especially Duke, who was, though I didn't know it at the time, fighting his attraction toward me.

CHAPTER 2

DUKE and I became lovers for the first time in June, 1973.

It was neither premeditated nor inevitable. It just happened, aboard the *Wild Goose*, while we were in Seattle on location for Duke's new film, *McQ*.

Even my presence in Seattle was—literally—the result of a freak accident. While shopping at Bullocks, Mary St John had tripped and suffered a broken shoulder. The healing process had been slow and painful, and when the time had come for her to join Duke in Seattle, she simply hadn't been up to the trip.

Although I regretted Mary's misfortune, I was thrilled about working on location with Duke, and bursting with excitement when a driver picked me up at the airport to take me to the Seattle Yacht Club, where the *Wild Goose* was anchored. I was assigned the lower cabin on the starboard side, which was to be my bedroom and office for the next few weeks. In addition to myself and the crew, Duke's friends Chick Iverson and John Derek were aboard, as well as his son Ethan. Pilar, however, had decided to forgo the trip preferring to take Marisa and Aissa, who was graduating from high school that month, to Peru to visit their grandmother. I'd known that Pilar had not joined Duke in Durango, Mexico, the previous November when he was filming *Cahill, U.S. Marshal,* and that her absence had set off a rash of gossip about 'marital problems.' Duke and Pilar had just shrugged it off, however, and shortly after Duke's return, Pilar had thrown a spectacular black-tie New Year's Eve party at the house.

Certainly Pilar showed no concern about my substituting for Mary in Seattle, and at that point it seemed to me that Duke didn't care one way or another, either—just as long as *someone* was there to look after things.

Duke wasn't exactly ecstatic about the script for *McQ*. He felt there were too many loose ends, that the story about a divorced plainclothes detective out to avenge the murder of a fellow cop was old hat, and that much of the dialogue was stilted. Actually, the only thing fresh about *McQ* were the location sites around Seattle, but, as Duke told me, 'I haven't made a movie in over six months, and this one is better than most of the junk they've been sending me.' He was impatient to get to work.

I, too, was eager for the shooting to begin. It would be a totally new experience for me, and an instructive one. Duke's first day of work took place in a run-down building in Seattle. I had been given a script and a call sheet, but I couldn't make head or tail of the latter. Duke was on call for only two lines that day, but when he left the room, I had no idea he was finished for the afternoon, and I remained where I was. Barney Fotheringham had to be sent back to get me and bring me to the car, where Duke, besieged by fans, was handing out autograph cards at a furious clip. He wasn't upset with me, because he knew I was a novice at this kind of thing. But I was upset with me. I learned very fast to be ahead of him, to carry a supply of autograph cards at all times, to wind my way through the crowds and be in the car as soon as he was ready to take off. Duke seemed to have infinite patience with and affection for his fans, and because he didn't want any of them to be disappointed, he always made sure he had a large supply of autograph cards on hand whenever there was likely to be a large crowd: on location, at a premiere, wherever. Those cards were as important to him as his makeup case and his guns. (He always used his own guns in his movies.)

The first few days on a movie location were exciting; then it became routine. Usually Duke left very early for makeup and wardrobe, and I always left with him. During the interminable waits between takes, I'd take dictation or attend to whatever matters needed taking care of. Duke was quite friendly with the cameraman, his personal wardrobe man, Luster Bayless, and all the rest of the crew. He never exerted his star power, but I began to notice that he became awfully annoyed whenever he noticed me chatting with Luster or, for that matter, with any of the *McQ* company. One day, in fact, he chewed me out for that: 'Look, I want you where I am—not out fraternizing with those guys.'

It was almost as if he were jealous. I loved it!

We had been shooting for a few weeks when Pilar popped in from Peru, bringing Marisa along with her. Duke seemed genuinely delighted to see her, then terribly disappointed and angry to discover Pilar didn't plan to remain. Marisa, however, had been so lonely for her father that Pilar had decided to allow the little girl to spend several days on location with Duke while she went to Carmel to play in a tennis tournament.

'If that's the way you want it,' Duke later told me he had said, adding, with great sadness, 'That's the way she wanted it.' I've often wondered if that wasn't the point when Duke felt his marriage was beyond salvation, although he said nothing more about Pilar's departure at the time.

He was, however, happy having little Marisa with him. He never missed a night to go into her room and wish her sweet dreams with a kiss, and in the morning he'd slip in to kiss her good-bye, even if she was still asleep. I marveled at, even envied, Duke's uninhibited display of affection toward his children, and theirs toward him.

One day Duke told me Marisa had asked him, the night before, 'Doesn't Miss Stacy like me?' When Duke had asked her why she had that impression, Marisa had replied, 'Well, she never kisses or hugs me.' I told Duke that because of *my* childhood, I still found it difficult to go around kissing and touching people, big or little, no matter how fond I was of them. Duke merely shook his head and said, 'We're just going to have to cure you of that hang-up.'

And that's what he did.

Midway through the shooting, Warner Brothers held a gala premiere of *Cahill, U.S. Marshal* in Seattle, to take advantage of Duke's presence there. To my delight, Duke asked me to join him, Chick Iverson, and some of his other friends at the premiere. I'd never been to such an event before, and it was a gloriously exciting evening, marred only by a band of Indians—or men pretending to be Indians—protesting outside the theater, claiming the movie was unfair to red men.

I can't tell you what the protests were about, however. In fact, I can barely remember anything about the movie itself. All evening, I was seated alongside Duke, and for the first time, I felt a kind of electricity between us. There was nothing overt, there were no looks or touches, but there was something there. The past few weeks, on location, we had been together a great deal, and our relationship had become considerably more informal than it had been in Newport. There had been a lot more time for jokes and chats, and for the first time, we had begun to feel really *comfortable* with each other.

Still—this was something else again. Maybe I was imagining it.

When the movie was over, our group headed for a charming restaurant Duke had discovered that carried Sauza Conmemorativo, his favorite brand of tequila. The margaritas flowed like wine, the wine flowed like wine, and we were all giddy by the time we drove back to the *Wild Goose*. Chick and the others headed back to their cabins, and I was about to head toward mine when Duke took me gently by the arm and escorted me topside to his stateroom. It seemed like the most

29

natural thing in the world to go with him.

I slept late into the morning, and by the time I awoke, Duke had left the *Goose* for a reception being given by Governor Dan Evans, of Washington. I remember luxuriating in Duke's magnificent king-size bed, remembering the night before, trying to convince myself I hadn't dreamed the whole thing. Duke's cabin was as representative of the man as was his house in Newport: huge, tasteful, comfortable. I decided that, since there, I'd take advantage of his private bathroom facilities. I washed my hair, showered, wrapped myself in a huge bath towel, then picked up my clothing, tucked everything under the towel, and silently prayed I could sneak back to my little cabin without anyone being the wiser.

No such luck. As I turned the corner I practically collided with Chick, who was engrossed in conversation with John Derek and the others. I was ready to die of embarrassment. There I was, barefoot, with my hair dripping wet, wrapped in Duke's very identifiable bath towel, with my clothes clutched to my chest. I didn't even try to explain my appearance, but no one seemed particularly surprised by it.

Oh, dear, they *know*, I thought. Actually, they neither knew nor suspected that I had spent the night in Duke's cabin. Had I been wearing the outfit I'd had on for the premiere, it would have been a dead giveaway, but I later learned they'd just assumed I'd been using Duke's facilities to bathe in greater comfort. Their casual attitude toward me was most reassuring.

After Duke returned from Governor Evans' reception, he was equally as casual, acting no differently toward me from the day before. Later that evening he headed for his stateroom alone, and I returned to mine, totally confused. What did it mean? Was that the end of it? A one-night stand? Was he feeling guilty? I know I was, to some degree, and worried, too. Would it affect my working relationship with Duke? Would I be able to face Pilar again?

There was no sense in worrying about these things. I'd have to let the future take care of itself.

Soon afterward, the *McQ* company moved to Ocean Shores, Washington, for a few weeks of shooting. The studio rented us apartments in a small hotel, and domestic chores—keeping an eye on Ethan, cooking dinner, tossing our clothes into the washer—were added to my secretarial duties, and I loved every minute of it. I was taking care of Duke and *his* family, *his* household, entertaining *his* friends—and what fun it was. We often had some of the fellows on the picture over for dinner and card games. On occasion we drank too much and stayed up so late that it was not always easy to get to the set the next morning, but we always did. And although Duke may have had, as he'd say, one helluva hangover, it never affected his performance.

I know that Duke's drinking habits have become part of the legend. One writer even insisted that he drank at least a quart a day for forty years, which was certainly not true while I knew him. Duke certainly liked to drink, and, as he said to me, 'I drink for comradeship, and when I drink for comradeship, I don't bother to keep count.' But he could go for weeks at a time without touching a drop if he felt so inclined, and he never drank during working hours—*never*. During the last year of his life, of course, he became allergic to liquor, couldn't even stand the smell of anything containing alcohol.

After our location work in Ocean Shores, the company returned to Seattle to wind up shooting, and since the *Wild Goose* was away on charter—Duke chartered it for several months of the year to help with the upkeep—Duke and I moved into a lovely house on Lake Washington. Our relationship continued in a strictly professional way on the set, but at the house it was much warmer than it had ever been in Newport. I loved just being with him. We found we could talk to each other about almost anything. He was curious in particular about my early life in Louisiana, a subject I

31

rarely discussed with anyone, since it was something I wanted to forget. I told him about my parents' little farm outside of Forest, Louisiana, however, and how I was sent out to work in the fields as soon as I was old enough. After a dismal adolescence I enrolled in what is now Northeast Louisiana State University in Monroe, some sixty miles from home, aiming for a teaching certificate because my parents thought teaching was the thing for a young girl to do in those days. I had had to get up before dawn to get to classes and had rarely been home before sunset. The first and only time I rebelled at the hours and threatened to leave college, my dad had said, 'Fine. Go back to bed and forget about school. When you wake up, you can come out in the fields and help me.' I woke up fast. I graduated from college and taught at a high school for a year, at the less-than-munificent take-home pay of $283.33 per month, before deciding that I didn't want to be buried in a small town forever. Through one secretarial job and another, I finally found myself in California, where the call from William Neuhauser awaited.

Duke was highly amused when I told him about my Jane Powell paper dolls and how I had dressed them from the ads in the Sears catalogue. That struck home. He told me that when he was very little, he used to read the catalogues cover to cover and circle all the things he wanted, things that, because of his family's poor financial condition, he was never able to get. 'I used to dream,' he confessed, 'that someday I'd have enough dollars to order everything in that damn catalogue. Catalogues became an obsession with me.' They remained so for the rest of his life.

He was also amused when I told him I'd developed a slight crush on him when I was nineteen and saw him in *North to Alaska* in 1960.

'I was in Shreveport, Louisiana, making *The Horse Soldiers* at the time,' he said, and laughed. 'Why didn't you call me?'

I replied, 'I didn't have your number. Why didn't you call *me*?'

'Because I didn't know someone like you existed,' he said.

Duke was less amused when I pointed out another coincidence. His 1941 movie *Lady from Louisiana* had been playing in our little movie house the month I was born, and my eighteen-year-old mother had seen it while I was kicking up a storm in her womb. Duke's reaction to that story: 'Damn it, Pat, I was only thirty-four when I made that film for Republic—the exact age my son Patrick is now. Where the hell have all those years gone?'

Years? I had been wondering where the last months had gone. Selfishly, I was hoping something, anything, would happen to delay completion of *McQ*. The thought of returning to Los Angeles depressed me. Everything was proceeding right on schedule, however, so much so that one afternoon Duke was even let off early.

'Come on,' he said, 'I want to pick up some things to take back home to the family.' A jeweler named Paul Friedlander was an old friend of Duke's, and we made his store the first stop. Duke picked up a couple of things, and we admired several other pieces, including a gorgeous opal pin in one of the showcases. 'Isn't that pretty?' I said, and walked on.

Later that afternoon, as we were driving back to Lake Washington, Duke handed me a small box and said, 'Here, this is for you.' It was the opal pin. I have no idea what it cost or how he had managed to buy it without my noticing it, but I was overwhelmed. It was my first gift from Duke.

'I'll never take it off,' I said impulsively.

Duke hesitated before replying, weighing his words so my feelings would not be hurt or my joy diminished. Then he said, 'Pat, I think it would be better if you didn't wear it to the office. I'd rather Mary didn't know about this. It might hurt her feelings to think I was favoring you, and that lady would know in a minute where that pin came from.'

Finally, the day I had dreaded arrived. Director John Sturges yelled, 'That's a wrap,' the crew applauded, then started packing their gear, and it was all over.

Some friend of Duke's who had flown up by private plane to visit the set had invited him to fly back with them; I was to return by commercial airline with Luster Bayless and some other members of the company.

After dinner that night, Duke and I returned to that enchanting house in Lake Washington. One last nightcap, one final toast to the completed film, and then, as I started to retire to my room, Duke came up alongside me, put his arms around my waist, and wordlessly led me to the master bedroom.

Back home, my job resumed its normal pattern. I made my twice-weekly trips to Newport with Mary St John, and my relationship with Duke returned to a strictly professional level.

I saw very little of Pilar, who was busier than ever with her tennis club, and I became aware that Duke seemed moodier than usual. Since we were rarely alone, I had no chance to ask if there was anything bothering him.

One day, though, after I had been down to the house with him, going through the mail, he walked me to the front door and said quietly, 'I miss you, Pat.'

'I miss you, too,' I replied. 'Guess we'll just have to go on another location. Find a script and let's go to work.'

To me, 'missing' meant far more than physical closeness. What I really missed were our long and open conversations, the times when he could talk to me about things he wouldn't necessarily talk about with others: the lack of good scripts; the shortage of money, how it seemed to be going out faster than it was coming in. We couldn't talk this way in front of Mary. I liked and admired Mary, and she was pleased by the way I was doing my job, but I'm sure she had ambivalent

34

feelings toward me. She couldn't have been overjoyed about being 'expendable,' a perfectly natural feeling considering all the years she had worked for Duke. Mary had wanted to retire and spend more time at home with her husband, had talked about it for years, but once she had made the decision irrevocable by hiring me, she found it difficult to make the break. And Duke, of course, could never say, 'Okay, you can go now.'

Not long after we got back from Seattle, Duke was shattered to hear that his old buddy and mentor, John Ford, had succumbed to stomach cancer at his home in Palm Desert. Ford had been seventy-eight, and ill for quite a while, and Duke had known it was only a matter of time before he died—had seen him only a little while before—but that didn't diminish the personal sense of loss. It was Ford who had hired Duke as a prop boy back in 1927, when Duke was still Marion Morrison, a big, shy, twenty-year-old who played football for the University of Southern California. Duke loved to tell about how, early on, Ford had tried to intimidate him in a roughhouse. Duke had calmly retaliated by kicking the director in the rear, forever earning his respect.

'Pappy,' as Ford's intimates called him, had given Duke bit roles in some of his early films, and it was he who had recommended Duke to his pal, director Raoul Walsh, when Walsh had been casting about for a leading man for *The Big Trail* in 1931. It was also Pappy who had rescued Duke from a career of quickie Westerns and awful B movies by casting him as the Ringo Kid in *Stagecoach* some eight years later. After *Stagecoach*, the combination of Wayne and Ford left an indelible brand on film history. Over the years Duke screened many of them for me, from *She Wore a Yellow Ribbon* and *The Searchers* to *The Quiet Man* and *Donovan's Reef*.

Once the news of John Ford's death was made public, on the afternoon of August 31, Duke's phone never stopped ringing; it seemed every reporter in the world wanted some kind of statement. I can't recall what Duke told the press that day. I can't forget what he said to me: 'It's an end of an era, a goddamn end of an era. No one's ever been able to equal him; no one ever will.'

I had met Mr Ford once, the previous March, when, at Duke's request, I had worked at the American Film Institute's Lifetime Achievement Award dinner in the director's honor. It had been my first major Hollywood function, and I had been thrilled to meet such people as Maureen O'Hara and Jimmy Stewart, as well as President Nixon. Mr Ford had been so touched by the tribute, and so appreciative of Duke's efforts in seeing that the two receptions before the dinner went smoothly. And now Mr Ford was gone.

Duke and Pilar were invited to the funeral, of course. Mary St John, who had been on many of the Ford-Wayne locations, also received a personal invitation, but because Duke and Pilar would be in a separate section reserved for family and intimates, because she was so distressed by the death that she didn't want to be alone, she asked me to accompany her. I don't think Duke and I exchanged more than a few words that afternoon, but I couldn't remember ever seeing him so somber.

When I reported to work a few days later, Duke's melancholic mood seemed to have worsened. He seemed terribly preoccupied, often losing his train of thought in mid-sentence and asking me to read back the preceding paragraph of a letter on which we'd been working.

When we'd finished for the day and Mary had gone to freshen up, he turned to me and, with a tortured expression in his eyes, said bitterly, 'Everything has to end, sometime or another. Nothing is permanent; only a goddamn fool would think anything is forever.'

Naturally, I assumed he was referring to John Ford and the glory days. And perhaps he was, to some degree. But it was more, much more than Ford's passing that had provoked the outburst, and it wasn't until two months after Ford's death that I learned the actual cause of Duke's depression.

CHAPTER 3

ON October 31, 1973, Duke told me that he and Pilar had decided to separate. The news was very shocking. There'd been some storm signals in the air, and Duke had been so moody lately, but I had no idea the situation was so serious. I wanted to find out more about it, but Duke offered only a few more details, and I felt it wise not to press him.

Both Duke and Pilar wanted their parting to be dignified and amicable in every respect. Pilar was to remain in the house on Bayshore Drive, I learned, together with Ethan, Marisa and Aissa, until the place she had taken in Big Canyon, ten minutes away, was ready for occupancy. That would be in early December, when Duke went to New York to accept the National Football Hall of Fame Award. Although the children would officially make their home with their mother, there were to be no limitations set on the time or number of holidays they could spend with Duke.

Duke would not discuss the impending divorce with the press. When his marriage to his second wife, Esperanza (Chata) Bauer, had ended, there had been a rash of headlines, with messy accusations flying in all directions. Duke wanted the break with Pilar to be quiet, out of respect for her and concern for the children.

Needless to say, I had an immediate attack of guilt: had I had anything to do with the breakup? I lived with that question for several weeks, until finally I got up the nerve to ask Duke, and he assured me that, no, the problems had been there long before I had entered the picture, and they would have continued even if I'd never been around, It was then that he told me about the previous separation, the family counselors, the lawyers. 'It was just inevitable, Pat,' he said. But that didn't make it any less sad.

Mary St John, who loved and was extremely loyal to Pilar, was very unhappy about the situation and made an effort to show no favoritism. Later she'd say, 'Mr Wayne misses having a woman in the house. He's very much a family man. He's also a one-woman man. He tried very hard to save the marriage to Pilar. I'll say that for him.'

When Duke returned home from New York on December 6, Pilar and all her personal effects, together with some items she and Duke had collected over the years and agreed upon, were gone. Duke didn't come back to an empty house, however. Ethan had remained for a few extra days in order to greet his dad at the door. Duke later told me he had been more thrilled by *that* than by the gold medal he had just received.

With Pilar gone, my next question was, Would I be next? Would it be embarrassing to have me around now—a young, single woman in the house? That didn't seem like Duke's way, and yet he had said nothing recently to indicate that the personal relationship that had ceased after Seattle would eventually resume. That December, when he insisted that I go ahead with my Christmas trip to Louisiana and handed me a thousand-dollar bonus check, I couldn't help wondering if it was a subtle way of letting me down easy, if I would then get a call from Mary saying, 'Things just haven't worked out.'

But, of course, I was inventing problems where none existed. When I came home after the holidays, he presented me with a small gold pendant and told me how much he had missed me. Then, early New Year's Eve, he asked me and my roommate, Peggy Reagan, to attend a small cocktail party with him at his friend Bill Chambers' house. It was obviously a kind of chaperoned 'date,' done that way to avoid gossip. Duke still wanted me.

Meanwhile, the press of his engagements continued. It was at about that time that Duke received what he called the 'most irresistible invitation' of his life. He was roaring with laughter when he showed me the letter. It was from James M. Downey, the retiring president of the satirical *Harvard Lampoon*.

> We've heard you're supposed to be some kind of legend. Everybody talks about your he-man prowess, your pistol-packing, rifle-toting, frontier-taming, cattle-demeaning talents, your unsurpassed greatness in the guts department . . .
> 'You think you're tough? You're not so tough.'

Then, after elaborating on the *Lampoon*'s contention that Duke was the 'biggest fraud in history,' Downey ended with a challenge for Duke to show himself and his new movie in Cambridge, 'the most traditionally radical, in short, the most hostile territory on earth.'

'Get out your pad, Pat,' Duke said. 'I'm going to give those young bastards the goddamndest surprise of their lives!'

This is what he replied:

> I accept with pleasure your challenge to bring my new motion picture *McQ* into the pseudo-intellectual swamps of Harvard Square. I was most happy to find that my age and balding head and gray hair had not made cowards out of the purported gentlemen of the mother college. May the Good Lord keep you well until I get there.
>
> JOHN WAYNE

After some discussion, the date of January 15 was decided on, which would fit in perfectly with Duke's schedule, since he was due in London a few days later to tape a Glen Campbell special and could book a direct flight from Boston.

I was to stay at home, minding the store, but before he left for Cambridge, he promised to call me immediately after the affair was over and let me know if he was 'still in one piece.' He was now beginning to have a worry or two about his decision to go—he would, after all, be a sitting duck—but it was too late to 'retreat in the face of the enemy.'

I remember waiting anxiously for his call, first at the office, then at my apartment, but there was not a word until about midnight, California time. Then the phone rang, and there was Duke, sounding exhilarated, and feeling no pain. 'Pat, I had the best damn time of my life. I want to tell you that after it was all over, they gave me a dinner at the *Lampoon*, these young guys, and they were such refreshing young men, goddammit, and they appreciated the fact that I had accepted their humor, and they really gave me a thoroughly enjoyable evening. I just got back to the hotel. They're gonna give me a transcript of the interview, and I'll send it back to you with a little surprise.'

Duke went on, filling in the details. He had ridden into Harvard Square atop a thirteen-ton Army personnel carrier manned by members of Troop D of the Fifth Armored Cavalry, 178th Infantry Brigade, Fort Devon, whose insignia proclaimed them the Black Knights. Some two thousand spectators had lined up to watch the 'invasion'; a dozen or so Indians had tried to block the procession; other unfriendly natives had pelted him with snowballs, and a few had even tried to throw themselves in front of the tank, before Duke had reached the assigned battleground—the Harvard Square Theater—where some sixteen hundred students had been ready for action.

'They really let me have it, Pat,' Duke told me, 'but I loved every goddamn minute of it. I wish you'd been here to share it with me.'

He wished?

The transcript, when it arrived, was all Duke had said it would be. No wonder he had got a standing ovation when he'd left the stage. The evening had opened with one student announcing, 'We all know what John Wayne stands for, what he has stood for all his life. But we invited him anyway.' And then the barrage of enemy salvos had started, fast and furious, for twenty-five minutes. Here are a few examples of how Duke handled himself in 'the most hostile territory on earth':

Q: Where did you get that phony toupee?
DUKE: It's not phony. It's real hair. Of course, it's not mine, but it's real.

Q: Is it true that your horse filed separation papers?
DUKE: He was a little upset when we didn't use him in the last picture.

Q: What did you use?
DUKE: Three good-looking women.

Q: What are your views on women's lib?
DUKE: I think they have a right to work anyplace they want to . . . as long as they have dinner on the table when you come home.

Q: Can you do an Ed Sullivan imitation?
DUKE: I'm having a hard enough time imitating people who are imitating me.

Q: Why do you refuse to allow midgets in your major films?
DUKE: It's too hard to find their mouths to punch.

Q: Has President Nixon ever given any suggestions for your movies?
DUKE: No, they've all been successful.

Q: What have you done with the Watergate tapes?

DUKE: If anybody is taping this show, I hope it's a Democrat, because the Republicans sure will lose it.

Q: Is it true that since you've lost weight, your horse's hernia has cleared up?
DUKE: No, he died and we canned him, which is what you are eating at the Harvard Club.

Q: Do you look at yourself as the fulfillment of the American dream?
DUKE: I don't look at myself any more than I have to, friend.

Duke went on to tell the student body, 'Contrary to a rumor circulating on campus, I will not appear as a *Cosmopolitan* centrefold—I have two big calluses—nor will I star in the first pornographic Western, *Last Tango in Tucson*.' Then he answered the last, and in my opinion the most sensible, question of the evening:

Q: How did they convince you to put up with all this?
DUKE: Well, I kinda like it. I'll tell ya, when I was a little boy, we had Halloween, in which you could tear things apart, and the Fourth of July, when you could blow your heads off. All the do-gooders have stopped all that, and I think you have to have a day when you can use up all the energy you wish . . . It's been a lot of fun.

Together with the transcript, Duke sent me the surprise: a trophy called the Brass Balls Award, presented by the *Lampoon* in recognition of 'outstanding machismo and a penchant for punching people in the mouth.' Duke thought that was funny, too.

From there he went on to London. From his first transatlantic phone call, I learned that the British press had welcomed him enthusiastically, and that, what with parties, interviews, salutes, and the like, he had been consuming far too much booze and getting far too little sleep. And that wouldn't be the end of it. After the Glen Campbell special was completed, Duke told me, he was to be feted at a big London press party and then at a gala at the American embassy before he was due back in California.

However, when he called again, I couldn't even recognize his voice. He was alarmingly hoarse, his breathing was ragged, and he had violent coughing spells throughout our conversation. He told me he'd come down with a cold after having gone from the frigid, dry climate of Boston to the frigid, damp one of London. He hadn't paid too much attention to it at first, but when he had started coughing up blood, his cold had been diagnosed as a viral infection, and the British doctor had insisted he remain in bed for at least four days.

'Don't worry, Pat,' he said, 'most of my scenes on the special have been taped, so I'll just take it easy for a few days and I'll be as good as new.'

Frankly, I couldn't have cared less about the special, and in spite of Duke's admonitions about not worrying, I was worried sick, knowing how he hated to renege on an invitation.

He called again on the eve of his departure for California. He told me he was still coughing some, but he felt as good as new. He didn't look as 'good as new,' though, when he arrived home. He looked awful. His 'viral infection'—although he was unaware of it at the time—had turned into walking pneumonia, and his chronic cough, which he shrugged off as a slight case of bronchitis, was playing havoc with a small area of his heart, a bit of 'plumbing' called a 'mitral valve.'

It would be four years before Duke would learn what it was that really ailed him.

CHAPTER 4

SOON after his return, Duke decided to make some changes in his business operations. He moved the Batjac offices from Paramount Studios to a suite on Wilshire Boulevard in Beverly Hills, and, much to our delight, I was to work full-time at the house on Bayshore Drive.

It didn't matter that I'd have to get up much earlier every morning to get from Marina Del Rey to Newport by nine A.M. All that mattered was that I would be seeing Duke *every* day. Mary St John, who was finally phasing herself out, would come only when urgently needed. Although Mary still found it difficult to make the final break, she'd reluctantly told Duke and me that she'd be leaving permanently that summer, as soon as Duke returned from England, where he'd be making his next film.

Life in Newport soon settled into a lovely routine. Even now I can remember the feeling of anticipation as I waved myself past the security guard stationed at the entrance to the Bayshore Drive colony: knowing that I'd be spending time with Duke, even if it was just going through the mail, made me happy.

And even after more than a year and a half, I was still enchanted by his house and everything in it. Duke often told me that he loved the surprised looks on the faces of first-time visitors. 'They always expect my place to look like a high-class tack room, stinking of leather and decorated with horseshoes. They probably expect to sit on saddles instead of chairs!'

There were, of course, some rare Western artifacts

in Duke's den, but they dominated neither that room nor the house. From its exterior there was little to distinguish Duke's home from many of the others along Bayshore Drive. A buff-colored wood fence enclosed a patio lushly planted with palms; huge, gorgeous ferns lined the walkway that led to the front door.

It's been said that a man's home reflects the man. Duke's home certainly did. With its many art objects—the two statues of Balinese women in praying attitude at the dining-room entrance; the exotic Chinese screens; the huge, square, red-lacquered coffee table in the living room—the house reflected a man of taste and intelligence and exuded a warm, lived-in feeling.

From my first visit, however, I always felt that if ten of the eleven rooms were to vanish, and Duke's den were to remain intact, that one immense room would tell the story of Duke's life. How can I begin to do it justice? The fine wood paneling, the fireplace, and the small collection of guns strengthened the feeling that this was definitely a man's room, yet on the wall-length shelf above the fireplace was Duke's prized collection of Hopi Kachina dolls. To the left of the fireplace, above the cabinet upon which his Oscar for *True Grit* rested, was what Duke referred to as his 'Fifty Years of Hard Work' wall, on which he displayed the honors and tributes he had received from all over the world. On that wall, too, beautifully framed, were the two tributes that I think meant the most: a poem written by Aissa when she was sixteen, as a gift for his sixty-fifth birthday, and another poem composed by one of his older daughters, Melinda, when she, too, was sixteen, commemorating Duke's forty-seventh birthday, in 1954. Aissa's poem read:

ONE MAN

One man, whose worth may sometimes
seem to be unknown
but whose height is taken:
One man who alone can stand fast

46

to his own ideas
but is never scorned:
One man is my father too,
for that 'one man' is you.

And from Melinda:

Sturdy as an aged oak tree,
This my father's strength might be.
But what I love of all daddy's parts
Is his most kind and generous heart.

There were many other things in that room: a hidden screen and projector for Duke's Friday-night screenings, to which he invited his friends; a theater-size popcorn machine; a 'pong' game; and of course, several large, comfortable sofas and chairs. At the far end of the room was the nook that served as his office, and eventually as mine. The office furniture itself was designed for a tall person, and I had to perch on books and pillows to reach the typewriter. Duke's chair was a foot or so away—and, believe me, it was his chair. No one else *ever* dared sit in it. Duke was the most generous man I ever met, but heaven help anyone who usurped *his* chair. He simply had a thing about it.

Much of the correspondence we received was of the usual sort—fan letters and requests for pictures—but included in it, too, were a great many letters from cancer victims or close relatives of cancer victims, people wanting advice and encouragement from Duke because of the lung cancer he had beaten in 1964. Duke gave these his special attention and kept the originals in a separate file. He'd write back to these people about his own experience, tell them 'not to forget that Man Upstairs,' and remind them that the best four-letter word was 'H-O-P-E.'

We also received some loonies at times. There was a fellow from Stockton, California, who would send letters addressed JOHN WAYNE/PALATIAL NEWPORT BEACH HOME, together with blank checks, or checks for

47

a million dollars, or credit-card applications. He would also write and profess his love for Aissa. We didn't answer those letters but kept them on file in case the guy ever surfaced and became dangerous.

I don't recall any threats to Duke's person or, for that matter, any kidnapping threats concerning the children. Duke never had any bodyguards around either him or the children. At the time of the Patty Hearst incident, he talked vaguely about taking out kidnap insurance, but I believe that was just a fleeting thought.

I think one of the oddest letters Duke received was from a lady who claimed she was Duke's illegitimate daughter. She wrote three or four times, but those letters were sent to Duke's attorney. Another girl claimed she was Duke's and Maureen O'Hara's daughter! I can't recall letters from would-be or discarded lovers, however. Maybe he received some of those in his earlier days but not during the time I worked with him.

At least that kind of fantasy would have been understandable, but a few women who wrote to Duke were really strange. For years there was an avalanche of mail from a woman back East who would send folded-up cigarette packages, gum wrappers, crumpled dollar bills, and all sorts of peculiar objects. Duke was amused at first but then got to the point where he didn't want to see that mail anymore: there was no way he could aid or comfort anyone that mentally disturbed.

Nor was there any way he could cope with a lady, whom I shall call Annie, who kept coming to the house in an effort to meet him. We never knew how she maneuvered through the Bayshore gate, but she did, and even rang the front doorbell a few times. Annie wrote daily. She'd start the letters telling him how much in love she was with him, and then she'd get progressively obscene. She'd write about how sure she was that she and Duke were meant to be together, that she was a real churchgoer and that God had told her all about it. She'd include a lot of intimate things about Duke, and go on to describe her 'wet dreams' and other X-rated items. Her letters were immediately recognizable: they were kissed with heavy lipstick. She even left a birthday cake on his doorstep one evening. We disposed of it immediately. Heaven knows what was in it!

And then, of course, there was the mail we filed under 'Requests.'

A great many people thought that Duke bathed in thousand-dollar bills, and they wanted some of the excess for themselves. Some of the letters were so pathetic that Duke would say, 'Oh, send her a hundred dollars.' This didn't sit too well with Duke's business manager, who thought it could start a chain reaction, and indeed in one case it did.

One lady wrote that she was in dire need of money to visit the grave of her son who'd been killed in the attack on Pearl Harbor. Duke sent the fare. Then she wrote back that she had been robbed. Another check. Then she had been hospitalized and had had to spend the money on doctor bills. Duke was a softy. 'Poor thing,' he told me. 'Let's send her another hundred.'

'Duke, you're being conned,' I said, but he simply wouldn't accept the fact. The letters were poignant and believable enough—but after three or four times?

Sometimes, when he didn't send money to those who requested it, we'd actually get abusive phone calls demanding to know why it hadn't been sent. We also received letters from complete strangers who would not only ask for something like an automobile but actually describe in detail the make and model they wanted. And there were hundreds of requests for his guns.

Worst of all were the people who stole from Duke. We tried to keep potted plants at the end of the dock, but they were always taken; the plants in front of the house would also mysteriously disappear. Once, even the mailbox vanished. Everyone wanted a John Wayne souvenir.

There was also a fair amount of hate mail regarding Duke's politics. Duke had a standard reply, and he *did* reply to those letters: 'You may disagree completely with what I say, but I will defend to the death my right to say it.' Nevertheless, he was often hurt by the letters.

'What bothers me most,' he told me, 'is that picture of me as an extremist. In my own mind, I'm liberal. I listen to every point of view, and then make up my mind. Isn't that what a liberal should do? They're just too pigheaded to see that.'

Duke's correspondence also included dozens of letters every week requesting his appearance at some benefit or other, or asking for the use of his name for a fund raiser. By now we had worked together long enough for me to determine whether or not he'd be likely to accept the invitation. I'd type up the response and give it to him for signature. He'd of course read the letter of regret before signing it, and a couple of times he said, 'No, I want to do *that*,' but it didn't happen too often. He was careful about the causes to which he lent his name. Having been badly burned a few times in the past, he would now do it only if it were an organization with which he was actively involved, and it was impossible for him to be actively involved in everything. It just seemed that he was.

Duke was involved in several business ventures as well, and I took pads of dictation related to them. He was all fired up about a company run by his friend Bill Chambers called Separation and Recovery Systems, which had to do with separating oil and water. Another friend of Duke's, Joe DeFranco, eventually became head of that company, and Duke and Bill went on to concentrate on another one, called DECO, the Duke Engineering Company. Duke, like everyone else, was concerned about an oil shortage, and Bill had come up with a process of liquefaction and gasification. They had started with oil shale, then gone on to coal, and finally to old tires. Duke explained to me that reclaiming and processing old tires yielded a top petro-chemical oil, plus a gas that could make a plant more self-contained. I have no idea how the system worked, but I visited the plant and did see oil coming from a complicated contraption of pipes. Duke's excitement about DECO was due in part to the fact that the system was pollution-free; there was no toxic waste to contaminate the air or the sewer systems. Duke kept a little bottle of oil from DECO in the den alongside his Oscar. I couldn't keep track of the dozens of letters Duke made me type to government officials in his attempt to interest them in his company. He was really so proud of what he and Bill were doing, but in addition to the ecological factor, he felt he could make some money with this undertaking.

Meanwhile, our relationship continued to develop. During the workday, it was still business as usual, but we began going out to dinner more and more frequently, sometimes alone, sometimes with his close friends, such as the DeFrancos and the Iversons, or his agent, Jack Gordean, and Jack's wife, Ruth. He also liked to have me join him for Sunday brunch at the Big Canyon Country Club.

And then, in late spring, Duke presented me with a real surprise. His next film, *Joe Battle* later renamed *Brannigan,* was due to start shooting in London in June, and I'd had only faint hopes of getting to go with him. One day, however, he turned to me and said, 'You know, I was a goddamn fool not to take you to London with me in January. I needed someone to look after me. So you better make sure your passport is in order, because you're coming with me. And if you behave yourself, I might even let you persuade me to take you to Paris.'

CHAPTER 5

OUR time in London marked a turning point in our relationship from which we never retreated. After London, there was never again any doubt: we were committed to each other; we were in love.

The trip started less than propitiously. Duke had gone ahead to Greece to take care of some DECO business and was planning to join me in London in time for my thirty-third birthday, on June 6. United Artists would make the hotel arrangements. When I arrived in London, however, I discovered to my dismay that the suite the studio had reserved for Duke at the Athenaeum Hotel and the small room they had taken for me were directly next to each other: a lovely personal arrangement but ideal ammunition for every gossip columnist in town.

I hurriedly switched my room for another, on the floor just above, and then took off back to the airport to meet Duke's plane. I was so excited I wanted to run into his arms, but the publicity people from United Artists had alerted the newspapers about his arrival, and it was such a mob scene I had to wait in the car until the reporters and photographers finally departed.

Duke was mad as hell about that, and he was only slightly less angry when he heard what I'd done with the rooms. 'Why in God's name did you do that?' he roared. 'What was wrong with them? Is there any law that says a man can't have his secretary nearby?' It was more than that, and Duke knew it, so he just let off some steam and let it drop.

As it turned out, changing rooms was almost more

52

trouble than it was worth. I was afraid to take the elevator to his floor in case I'd be seen, so through our stay there I made stealthy trips through hallways and down the back stairs between his floor and mine: scenes right out of a French farce. Duke thought the whole thing was crazy, but there was no point in trying to get my original room back, even if we wanted to, because we were just marking time until the house Duke had rented for the summer became available.

That first day, we had barely stepped into his suite when he threw one of his suitcases onto the bed and opened it up to show me what he'd brought. It was packed to the rim with birthday presents for me: Greek blouses, a jacket, an antique silver belt, a gold ring, and an exquisite dress, which he wanted me to wear at a big 'surprise' birthday dinner that night. I was slightly disappointed, having hoped we'd be alone his first night in London. But Jack Gordean had flown into town for the start of the film, and Duke had invited several other friends for the celebration, and, as it turned out, we had a great time.

Ten days later we moved into a charming house at 20 Cheyne Walk, in Chelsea. Although it was two hundred years old and there were fifty-four stairs (I counted them!) leading to my room, it was one of the few houses in London with a swimming pool, a feature that appealed to Duke's sense of the incongruous. The privacy appealed to me most: no more sneaking up and down hotel stairs.

It was expensive enough, though. During the filming of *Brannigan,* Duke was given a per diem allowance by the studio, as was usual. He received fifteen hundred dollars a week for all his expenses and had to account for every penny. There was never anything left over. The rent on the house alone was the equivalent of twenty-five hundred dollars a month.

The accounts were part of my job. In London, as on every other location I was to be on, I had to keep a record of *everything* Duke spent. He was no good at keeping receipts, so whenever I was with him, I'd pick them up and file them safely away. In London I had to do conversions on a daily basis because of the fluctuations in the British pound against the American dollar. That was a job in itself. In addition, the balance in Duke's personal checking account was never particularly high. In fact, we were never exactly sure what was in the account until the statement arrived, since Duke had an exasperating habit of never recording a check he had written. At home he had checkbooks all over the house, and when he needed a check, he'd tear one out of whatever book was handy. If I'd have to pinpoint my greatest failure as Duke's secretary, it would be my inability to balance his checkbook. I think a computer would have blown its circuits trying to do *that*.

The house at Cheyne Walk came equipped with a maid and butler, a black Rolls-Royce, and a chauffeur named Danny. One rainy night after we had just settled in, Duke suggested we have Danny drop us at the White Elephant, a wonderful restaurant we had discovered the week before by the banks of the Thames. 'Why have Danny wait around in this storm? We'll get a cab home,' Duke said. Wonderful! Just Duke and me in the most romantic restaurant in town.

Because of the storm, the restaurant was nearly deserted. We had a cozy window table, and we started dinner on a splendid note: caviar, which we washed down with ice-cold vodka. Suddenly, however, I was seized by violent stomach pains. I excused myself and raced to the powder room, where I was one very sick lady; then I returned to the table, sure I'd be okay if I just ordered some clear chicken broth. A few seconds later, however, I had to excuse myself a second time. After the third trip upstairs, Duke said, 'I think I better get you home.'

It took nearly an hour to find a cab in that rain and fog. It took longer than that to reach a doctor after we arrived home. In desperation Duke called the Athenaeum and persuaded the hotel doctor to rush to Cheyne Walk, where he diagnosed severe food poisoning. It wasn't the caviar but some bad buttered clams I had had earlier in the day. I felt so awful, I wanted to die.

Duke and the doctor remained with me all that night. I remember telling the doctor that I had to get up, had to go to work the next day, that Duke had to go to work—shooting had started the week before—but Duke just hushed me up and sat on my bed until five A.M., when, after some medication, I finally fell asleep. After he got reassurance that I'd be all right in a day or so, Duke went back to his room, changed clothes, and went off to Tower Bridge, where he was filming that day, without even an hour's sleep. He called me several times that afternoon to see how I was feeling, and although I protested that I was much better and could get down to the set, he said if I dared come down to the Tower after what I had been through, he'd 'behead' me personally. It wasn't until the next day that he let me go back to work, and even then he made me take it easy.

The shooting of *Brannigan* proceeded uneventfully. As a movie, *Brannigan* was not particularly noteworthy. Duke played a Chicago detective sent to England to bring back a racketeer escaping from a grand-jury indictment. As Duke described it, 'It's the same old Western plot brought up to date. The out-of-town gunman moves in to help the sheriff round up the renegade bad man, except this time he does it in London instead of Monument Valley.' Duke seemed to be in excellent health, and at sixty-seven he did action scenes that would tax the strength of men half his age. Midway through the filming, however, there was a development that taxed if not his strength then at least his patience—and mine.

He got a call from Pilar. Marisa, Ethan, and Aissa missed him a great deal, and she was planning to bring them to England for a short visit. And his son

Michael and Michael's wife, Gretchen, would also be in London at that time: a real family reunion.

What could Duke say? The house at Cheyne Walk was large enough to accommodate everyone—everyone but me! Propriety demanded my temporary eviction. I was moved bag and baggage to the Penta Hotel, where most of the crew were staying, and then I had to have the car take me straight to Heathrow to meet Pilar's plane, escort the family back to Cheyne Walk, and see that Pilar was comfortably ensconced in what I regarded as *my* bedroom.

Of course, I was with Duke all day on location, and occasionally I'd come to the house for dinner, but most of the time the evenings were lonely. I would have dinner in my room and just read or watch television. None of the crew invited me to do anything. They all knew that Duke and I had a special relationship, and so they stayed away. In fact, one crew member came right out with it: 'Pat, we all know how you and Duke feel about one another. We can see it just from the way you look at each other. It shows.' So our secret wasn't quite as secret as we thought, but still we played the game.

One day Luster Bayless noticed how miserable I was and invited me to go off on a shopping expedition with him. It was a lot of fun, but another of Duke's aides noticed us leaving the Penta together and, astonishingly, proceeded to tell Duke, 'Luster is making time with your secretary.' Duke was furious. He called and accused me of having something going with Luster. I was horrified. I tried to explain that Luster had simply been going to Harrod's, since I had had nothing to do, he had asked me along.

'What do you mean you had nothing to do?' Duke demanded. 'You were supposed to take the kids to see the Tower of London.'

'But, Duke, Pilar phoned and told me that *she* wanted to take them to the Tower, and so I wouldn't be needed.'

'Is that so? Well, they were at the house all day!'

The following morning at work, Duke was still making noises about Luster and me and my not taking the kids to the Tower, and I simply handed him a copy of that morning's London *Times*. The day before, a terrorist had planted a bomb in the Tower, and it had gone off, causing some damage. I said quietly, 'You should be awfully glad we didn't go.'

But he wasn't listening.

'You didn't take them because you were out all day living it up with Luster.'

Just then he was called off to do a scene, and we were very cool to each other for the rest of the day. But that wasn't the end of it.

The next morning, Duke invited both Luster and me to dinner at the house. Obviously he wanted to see us together, to judge for himself if anything had been going on. He had said nothing to Luster about our so-called date.

What a crazy night! All through dinner Duke kept studying Luster and me, and none too subtly. Pilar meanwhile, was trying to make up *her* mind about Duke and me. A couple of weeks before, Duke and I had used a break in the shooting to pay a quick visit to Ireland, and Pilar knew all about it. The mouths had obviously been busy. Finally, she turned to me. 'Well, Pat,' she said, 'what did you think of Ireland?'

I gulped, and tried to think of something innocuous to say. 'I remember it was brown and gray,' I finally replied. 'The countryside was green, but the people were all dressed in either brown or gray.' It wasn't the most scintillating observation, but she had made her point—that she *knew*—and so made no further comment.

It was an awkward, uncomfortable evening. Later Duke admitted that Michael had told him he thought Duke had embarrassed Pilar by taking me to Ireland, and I couldn't help wondering if Michael was right. Had I misread the situation? Was the separation over, after nine months? Had Pilar come to England to try for a reconciliation? The day before Pilar was to fly home, I got up the courage to say to Duke, 'If you want to go back, so you can have your family around you all the time, do it. Don't worry about me. I'll understand. I'll be okay.'

But he only replied angrily, 'Don't ever talk about it again.' Pilar left the next morning, and I returned to Cheyne Walk.

Duke knew how rough those few weeks had been on me, and by now he was quite contrite about his reaction to the gossip about Luster. He wanted to show me the best time I had ever had in my life, and of course he knew just how to go about it.

All my life I had dreamed of going to Paris. I had always had a predilection for things French—architecture, clothes, food—but the closest I had ever got to the city of my dreams was the French Quarter of New Orleans.

Paris was just an hour away, but because of Duke's six-day-a-week work schedule, it could have been on an other planet. It had only been due to some very persuasive arm-twisting that he had been able to get the time off to go to Ireland. So I'll never forget the morning when I joined Duke in his dressing room at Shepperton Studios and, with a sly grin on his face, he said, 'You've been dying to go to Paris. Okay, let's go to Paris! Book a room for us at the George V.'

I was too excited to make much sense. 'But how can we—the shooting—they won't—'

'I just got word they're not going to need me for a couple of days, so why hang around? If I don't get you to Paris, I'll never hear the goddamn end of it.'

Duke didn't want the studio to know of his plans. 'They might have a change of mind at the last moment,' he said. 'So call some travel agent, book a flight for tonight, and let's go.'

I got on the phone immediately. There was no problem about airplane tickets, but there was a problem about a room. It was the height of the tourist season. The George V was filled to capacity; so were the Ritz and the Plaza-Athénée—all of them. 'But it's for John Wayne,' I told the travel agent. She was unimpressed.

During the tea break I told Duke the bad news.

'To hell with that crap,' he replied. 'We're going to Paris, even if we have to sleep on a park bench!'

After our plane landed at Orly Airport, Duke ordered the cabbie to drive directly to the George V. When we arrived at the hotel, he asked to speak to the manager. Five minutes later we were escorted royally to Suite 152, just about the most gorgeous suite I had ever laid eyes on.

I guess *someone* was impressed with John Wayne.

I'll never forget looking out the window that first morning and seeing our hotel reflected in a nearby glass building, or the heady excitement of driving leisurely along the Champs-Élysées, under the Arc de Triomphe, and through the narrow, hilly streets of Montmartre.

My excitement was obviously contagious. During the drive Duke held me very tight and said, 'You know, I've seen it all before, but I love seeing it again now through your eyes. It's wonderful being here alone with you.'

Thousands of poems and songs have been written about the City of Light, but the one that kept going through my head that day was a song by Cole Porter: 'Paris Is for Lovers,' he wrote, and he was right. It *is* for lovers—all of it—and I think that during that weekend in Paris, Duke and I became lovers in the deepest sense of the word.

That first night, he went out of his way to give me the most romantic evening of my life. He booked a window table for dinner at La Tour d'Argent and ordered Dom Perignon and all the fanciest things on the menu, including the duck for which the restaurant was famous. I could hardly eat, though. I was so excited I just wanted to gaze around: at the restaurant, at Paris, at the magnificent view of Notre-Dame cathedral in all its brightly lit splendor. Duke, however, wasn't about to allow any of the duck to go to waste, so he reached over and helped himself to what was left on my plate.

Oh, how he loved to eat . . . then. He considered good food and fine wine among the great pleasures of life. How could either of us foresee the day when he'd consider himself lucky to be able to finish a dish of tapioca pudding.

After dinner Claude Terrail, the owner, took us on a private tour of the wine cellars. It was all so romantic; we had such a wonderful time I wanted to get back to the hotel and fall into Duke's arms. But things didn't quite work out that way. Duke never should have eaten my portion of the duck. He ended up sick to his stomach most of the night, and very apologetic about ending the evening on such a downbeat note.

Even that couldn't spoil our weekend, though. By morning Duke was raring to go on a walking tour of the city, and it seemed we went everywhere. When we started up the Eiffel Tower, however, we got no farther than the third landing. At that point Duke said to me, 'Do you really want to go to the top?' When I told him that it really didn't matter, he sheepishly admitted that he had a fear of heights, and I confessed that my stomach was getting jumpy just looking down from landing number three. Who needed the top of the Eiffel Tower? We were high just being together and in Paris.

When we returned to street level, we hailed a cab and asked to be taken to Fouquet's for lunch. The driver didn't speak English, and he kept asking Duke something, we didn't know what. Duke thought he wanted his autograph, so he handed him an autograph card. A few blocks later the driver stopped another cab and showed him the card, and we thought he wanted his buddy to get an autograph, too. As it turned out, Duke had been mangling the pronunciation of the restaurant, and the driver hadn't the foggiest idea where we wanted to go, and when Duke had handed him the card, he thought it was an address card, which, naturally, he couldn't make head or tail of. It took a few minutes to unravel it all, but when the light bulbs finally went on in our heads, the cabby got us there in record time—those Parisian cabbies live up to their reputation for being wild drivers—and we had a fabulous lunch.

We had a light dinner at the hotel that night and retired early. It was then that Duke and I really admitted to each other that we had a special relationship going. We had love to give, and we gave it and gave it, freely and without guilt. As a lover Duke was affectionate, considerate, and gentle. If there weren't fireworks bursting in the air, we didn't care. Neither of us was a kid. We were mature enough to realize that there were more powerful elements involved in lovemaking than these described in popular novels. Together we achieved total communication, something that drew us closer to each other as human beings. It was so easy to love Duke.

On Sunday afternoon we checked out of the George V, and Duke hired a car and driver to take us to a picturesque inn somewhere out in the French country-side. We had a beautiful lunch there and then went straight to the airport to catch our plane back to London—reluctantly. I cried as we left the ground, and Duke was reassuring me. 'Cheer up, we'll come back,' he said. If only we could have.

When we arrived at Cheyne Walk, there were a dozen messages from the production company. They had gone frantic trying to find us, since we hadn't told anyone of our plans, and were practically ready to have the *real* Scotland Yard go looking for us.

Duke phoned the director, Douglas Hickox, demanding, 'What the hell's going on? You said you didn't need me until Monday, so I took off for a few days. What's the beef?'

Actually there had been no problem, until a production assistant had decided to phone Duke to tell him about some minor change. When Duke hadn't phoned back after the fourth, fifth, and sixth phone calls, panic had set in. Duke was actually quite amused by the whole affair. 'There's a kidnapping gimmick in the script, so those guys probably thought we'd been kidnapped or something, or were lying dead in a ditch in the provinces. I wouldn't be a bit surprised if they spent the whole weekend trying to figure out how to end the picture without me.'

He was at the studio at six the next morning. He never did tell them we had gone to Paris: 'None of their damn business.' He did, however, promise to let them know his whereabouts the next time he took off.

As it turned out, there was no next time. It was all work the next few weeks, six days a week. Doug Hickox had saved a big car-chase scene until last, just in case of an accident. It was a complicated scene shot on a barren field twenty miles outside of London, and although it was dangerous, both Duke and his co-star, Judy Geeson, refused to use doubles. Finally, on August 23, *Brannigan* was in the can. Duke sent me home early that day to cook his favorite cheese soufflé for the party he was giving for the cast and crew back at the Athenaeum Hotel. He had chili flown in from the States, there was an open bar, and a wonderful time was had by all.

Duke and I left London the next day. On the long flight home I was exposed to one of dear Duke's wackier displays of humor. As we wended our way to the first-class cabin, he started whistling Dimitri Tiomkins's very identifiable theme music from *The High and the Mighty*—in which Duke had played the pilot of a crippled airplane past the 'point of no return'—and he kept whistling it intermittently until we landed. Naturally, many of the passengers recognized Duke and the music, and knew the plot of the movie, and some of them were amused—but I don't know if they all were. It did present a somewhat unsettling image.

It was a stunt Duke would pull every once in a while from then on, until a few years later, when we had a near miss on a private airplane coming in for a landing in Arizona. After that, he no longer found his *High and Mighty* gag quite as hilarious.

The rest of the flight from London to California was delightful. And somewhere around the point of no return, Duke and I reached a tacit understanding that we would 'be together'—all the time and exclusively. I'd continue as his secretary, of course, but after five P.M. I'd be *his* girl, and no one else's.

'You're the only lady I want in my life, Pat,' Duke said quietly.

That was all I needed to hear.

CHAPTER 6

AS much as Duke and I had enjoyed Europe, we were
happy to come home again. And as much as I had
liked and respected Mary St John, I was secretly relieved
that she was gone.

Now Duke and I could express our feelings more
freely. Duke made sure I knew every day that I was
loved, with hugs and kisses and looks. I'd tell him, 'I
feel that I'm the luckiest girl in the world,' and he'd
reply, 'I'm lucky, too.' I said to Duke once, teasing,
'You gave Mary St John twenty-eight years: I expect
the same.' And he looked at me and said, 'The same,
Pat, and more.' He was so gentle and giving and
concerned.

There were many times when I wished his divorce
from Pilar would be finalized, so I wouldn't have to
worry about what people thought, but Duke never
seemed to care about public opinion. After work he
took me along as his date whenever he met close
friends. We'd have brunch every Sunday at the Big
Canyon Country Club and play cards or backgammon
throughout the lazy afternoons with his pals. He made
no secret of his affection for me in front of the younger
children, who were in and out of the house all the
time.

He loved Aissa, Ethan, and Marisa so. Here he was,
sixty-seven years old, and seeing these youngsters
grow up, day by day. He loved his older children, too,
but because he had been struggling to make a name
for himself while they were growing up, and was always
off somewhere working, he had never been able to

spend as much time with them as he'd wished during that special period of their lives. He often mentioned how much he regretted that.

I was never certain how the older Wayne children felt about me. Duke once remarked that he thought they'd resented any woman he'd become attached to after his divorce from their mother, Josephine, but I don't know if that was so. Michael had been openly hostile about our trip to Ireland, but the only other comment Duke ever repeated to me was when Michael said, 'She has good legs.'

Early on, there were moments when I felt jealous of all the loving attention the children received, but I quickly dismissed these feelings. I had him with me more than they had. I had him all day when they were in school or with Pilar. They'd rush into the house and say, 'Hi Dad; I love you,' and give him a kiss, and he would continue with his business, but just knowing they were there made Duke happy. Initially, I had worried about their reaction to Duke's kissing me or hugging me in their presence, but they seemed just to take it for granted. Duke had taught his children that expressing affection openly was the most natural thing in the world.

We remained in Newport for slightly less than a month, and then he had to pack and leave for yet another location. *Rooster Cogburn*, the sequel to Duke's Oscar-winning *True Grit*, was scheduled to start filming in Grants Pass, Oregon, early that fall, and Duke's formidable leading lady was to be none other than Katharine Hepburn.

Miss Hepburn had been in London when we'd been there, and had come over especially to introduce herself to Duke one afternoon when he had been filming in Piccadilly Circus. He had liked her immediately, and they had expressed their amazement that they had never met, let alone worked together, before. When they finally did get together, though, the chemistry between them was obvious to everyone.

65

Would that it had been so between Duke and the director, Stuart Millar. Miss Hepburn had tried to warn Millar. 'I don't envy you,' she'd said early on. 'You know, of course, that you are working with three bullies'—the third being producer Hal Wallis. It did no good, though. To be fair, with the possible exception of Douglas Hickox, Duke never got along with any of his directors during the time I was with him. Duke had worked with a lot of giants in the field, and he was a notorious perfectionist; if he felt someone—actor, crew member, or director—had not properly prepared himself or didn't know what he was doing, or was otherwise wasting people's time and money, he chewed him out good, and made sure everyone else knew what he thought, too. He was not always the most popular man on the set. In this instance things degenerated so far he even called the director—forgive me, Mr Millar—a 'six-foot-six sonuvabitch no-talent,' and Hal Wallis offered to replace him if it would make Duke happy. Duke said no. 'What difference does it make who they get?' he said to me. 'Kate and I will do what we want anyway.' To tell the truth, the two of them *were* the whole show.

The story line of *Cogburn* was more *African Queen* than *True Grit*. The booze-soaked ex-marshal meets the reverend's spinster daughter, and the odd couple join forces in pursuit of a gang of murderous desperados who have ambushed a cavalry detachment and stolen a wagonload of nitroglycerine—hence Cogburn's involvement—and shot down her father and murdered some converted savages. Duke was aware of script deficiencies even before he began the film, but he felt they could be overcome by spirited performances.

Certainly he and Miss Hepburn gave their all, and their performances were helped in no small way by the matchless personal rapport that developed from the first week on. At first everyone was apprehensive about their working habits. Miss Hepburn demanded a closed set: no visitors, and *definitely* no press hovering about. Duke, however, always enjoyed having friends around watching him work, and he preferred to conduct interviews on the set between takes or at lunch.

Publicist Jack Casey was burdened with the unenviable task of working out the problem. He approached Duke first.

'Duke, I don't know how to tell you this, but we can't get Hepburn to come out on the set with all these newspaper people you invited around. You know she has a thing about that.'

'Relax,' he told Casey. 'I'll talk to her.'

He went to Miss Hepburn's trailer and asked if she'd really mind *his* having them on the set, if they promised they wouldn't bother *her*. Well, she said, she guessed that would be all right—as long as they didn't come around her, mind.

Well, the upshot of that, of course, was that the reporters would wander over, and soon she'd have to join in, too, just for the fun of it. Duke would say something to tease her, and she'd just have to answer back, and before the reporter knew it he'd have pages of good copy, brimming with affection and playfulness.

This was especially evident when *People* magazine sent a team to Oregon for a cover story on them both. Duke and Miss Hepburn were exceedingly vocal about their admiration for each other.

Said Miss Hepburn about Duke, 'He has confidence in himself, which gives him enormous charisma. He's quick; he's sensitive. He knows all the techniques. I think he's an awfully good actor and a terribly funny man. We laugh all day. What a goddamn funny personality.'

To which Duke responded, 'I've never in my life worked with a woman who had the smell of drama that this woman has. She's so feminine—she's a man's woman.'

Much later, Miss Hepburn would confide to me privately. 'He reminded me so much of Spencer.'

My own relationship with Miss Hepburn was friendly

but not chatty. Between scenes she usually concentrated on her lines, and I knew better than to interrupt her. She always had a warm greeting and a smile when she saw me. It never occurred to me to wonder at the time if she was wondering if I was Duke's girl, his secretary, or both. We tried to keep everything very professional on location. But she knew; she knew all along. Two years ago I went to see her in a play in Los Angeles and went backstage to say hello. She gave me a great big hug and said, 'I know what you have gone through. But you kept him going. He loved you so much.' It brought tears to my eyes.

While Duke was working at Grants Pass, we stayed at a small motel not far from the shooting site, but in mid-October the location shifted to the picturesque and rugged forest outside of Bend, Oregon. Since we were to remain there until the movie was completed, Duke rented a house at nearby Sun River. I think it may have been the most perfect house we ever lived in while on location: big rooms, the walls all lined in cedar, a kitchen-dining area overlooking the patio and pool. I set up a little office in the house in order to cope with the piles of mail being forwarded from Newport.

Unlike on *McQ* and *Brannigan,* when Duke had had to work all day, every day, his scenes were now scheduled in such a way that he could have an entire morning or afternoon or even a couple of days all to himself, and definitely no work on weekends. We had a wonderful Israeli couple working for us, but because they observed the Sabbath strictly, they left before sundown on Friday, and Duke gave them the rest of the weekend off. There was a barbecue pit on the sun deck, and I became chief cook and bottle washer—and how I loved it! Usually we just relaxed, soaked up the sun, played cards, or talked. Duke welcomed any opportunity just to lounge around without his toupee. He was still a very handsome man without it, and he never wore it when he was with close friends, but when we went shopping or out to lunch, he always wore a cap, to preserve the image, he said. I remember shortly before we left for Oregon, Barry Goldwater's little grandson, who lived across the street, spotted him and said, 'Hi, Johnwayne [one word]. What happened to all your hair?' Duke was speechless for the moment, but he told me later, 'Dammit, Pat, if I had only been thinking, I would have told him an Indian scalped me. He would have been so excited!'

By now Duke was missing the children again, so he phoned Pilar to ask if Marisa and Ethan could join him for a long weekend, to which Pilar readily agreed. It was on this trip that Marisa got the nickname 'Nine Iron', though the circumstances were far from funny at the time.

Soon after she arrived, Duke decided to show her how to hit a golf ball. I was in the house at the time. His big mistake was in standing directly behind her. He told her to 'follow through' on her swing, which she did, and the iron hit Duke right above the eye. He was completely knocked out, and Ethan said later he looked 'just like a chicken bouncing around ready to fall.' Marisa, who was only eight, was totally devastated and blamed herself all day for hurting Dad. When they returned to the house, we called a doctor immediately. The doctor stopped the bleeding, cleansed the wound, and sewed it up with eight butterfly stitches so as not to leave a scar. He left instructions with me that Duke was to keep an eye patch on for the next several days. That wasn't difficult to do, under the circumstances, since the character Rooster Cogburn wore an eye patch, and I doubt if anyone who saw the picture was aware that in some scenes Cogburn's famous patch was several sizes larger than in others. Hal Wallis was lucky. Duke had been hit in the left eye—the 'correct' eye. Had the iron hit him in the right eye, moviegoers might have been subjected to a real oddity: the mystery of the moving eyepatch.

'Be grateful for small favors,' I told Duke.

'Not so small,' he replied. 'The doc told me if the club had hit one eighth of an inch either to the right or left, I might have been a dead man.'

In spite of the accident, work went on as usual. Katharine Hepburn insisted on doing her own riding, which scared Duke a great deal because he felt she really couldn't ride all that well. She agreed to have a stunt girl do the very fast long shots only after Duke told her that *he* was using a stunt man for those shots. 'No one's going to notice the difference, and I don't have to prove anything anymore, and neither do you.' Everyone breathed easier after that.

It was about this time that Duke decided to hold a lavish, belated birthday dinner at the house for Hal Wallis. Mr Wallis' birthday had actually gone by several days before, while we had still been at Grants Pass, but there the facilities at the motel had hardly been meant for gracious entertaining.

Several members of the company were invited, including Katharine Hepburn, of course, even though Duke had been warned that she never went out. Miss Hepburn thanked Duke for the invitation but begged off with the expected 'I never go out socially.'

'So I've been told,' Duke replied. 'But I just wanted you to know you're invited. And the invitation holds.'

The following day Miss Hepburn approached Duke, and asked if he'd mind if she came by for just a few minutes, out of respect for Hal, and if she could bring her secretary, Phyllis.

'Of course,' he said. 'Bring anyone you wish.'

Later in the afternoon Miss Hepburn came by again and asked if she could bring her *brother-in-law,* who was in town for a visit. 'It'll only be for a few minutes. I can't stay longer than that.'

'Yes, Sister, I told you,' he said, using his pet nickname for Miss Hepburn. 'There will be plenty of food for everyone.'

That evening, precisely on time, Miss Hepburn

arrived with her secretary and her brother-in-law, and the first words out of her mouth were, 'Remember, I'll only be here a few minutes.'

She walked in the door, and the first thing she did was pick up a painting of an Indian that both Duke and I had disliked but had done nothing about. She noted how awful it was, and turned its face to the wall. Why hadn't we thought of that?

The second thing she did was to head for the clams, shrimp, and duck ragout that Duke had flown in from Seattle. She filled up her plate, and before we had time to say how sorry we were that she couldn't stay and eat with us, she was partaking with gusto. Of course, the punch line is that she was practically the last person of all to leave that night. For months afterward Duke would tell the story to anyone who would listen. It was the highlight of his evening.

Miss Hepburn was also with us a few weeks later at Hal Wallis' house, but this time the evening was not so amusing. That was the night that Duke was coughing so hard and having such a terrible time breathing that we had to send our driver back to the house to get the small, green, ball-shaped oxygen tank we kept with us in case of emergency.

Duke had started taking the tank with him on location after the lung operation in 1964—high altitudes could be rough on a man with one lung—but he had never really used it all that much. For a little while now, however, he had been experiencing shortness of breath. He attributed it to the dust and cold, but he'd have to ride his horse from one location spot to another, even if they were only a short distance apart. It started to get so bad, and the dryness began to bother him so much, that we put a vaporizer in his bedroom hoping the moist air would bring some relief, and it did seem to help a little. That night at Hal Wallis', though, as we were waiting, Miss Hepburn took me aside and said, 'You better get him to a doctor as soon as possible and find out what's wrong with him. That's no ordinary

71

cough.'

Duke's coughing spell eventually abated, however. The oxygen relieved his breathing problem, and Duke wanted to get on with the film, which had to be wound up before the Oregon snow fell. I suggested to Duke he follow Miss Hepburn's advice, but he wouldn't hear of it. 'Damn it, I'm okay. Pat, It's just the air here. It'll go away.' And he wouldn't let me bring it up again.

He wouldn't complain about how much pain his knee was causing, either. The knee problem was the result of a freak accident that had occurred while he was working on a raft sequence. There had been guns and shells aboard the raft, and Duke had tripped on them, banging his knee. He dismissed the pain as only temporary, the natural effect of a bad bruise. It wasn't until he visited the doctor after our return to Newport that an X ray showed damaged cartilage that would require surgery to repair.

Miraculously, *Rooster* wound up right on schedule. To celebrate the occasion, I told Duke that after months of flitting about in slacks on the set, I would wear my prettiest dress on the final day of shooting. He seemed indifferent. So did everyone else when I arrived on the set—and throughout the afternoon. In fact, the crew went out of their way to avoid looking at me, though from the corner of my eye I noticed a few guys staring at my knees in a rather peculiar way. My dress wasn't transparent; my slip wasn't showing—I was totally confused. It wasn't until afterward that I found out what had happened. Before I had arrived on the set, Duke had spoken to the crew and requested that they make no comment about my wearing a dress or about my legs, because I had a fake leg, which was usually covered by my pants. Another of his practical jokes—and everyone took him seriously. I could have killed him, but he thought it was hilarious. 'Now you can see what a really good actor I am,' he said.

The picture was over, and for Duke the joy of going

home was tempered by the sadness of bidding good-bye to Katharine Hepburn. But at that point neither of them felt it would be their only film together. The picture ended with Rooster and Eula saying, poignantly, 'Someday . . .' and Hal Wallis was contemplating a sequel to the Cogburn saga, to be titled *Someday*.

Someday, however, was never to come, for many reasons. Duke was dissatisfied with the script ideas; the box-office receipts and reviews of *Rooster Cogburn* turned out to be nothing to crow about, and Universal Studios quietly backed away from the project.

But the Wayne-Hepburn mutual-admiration society continued. He discovered that she adored umbrellas, and whenever he spotted a unique parasol, he bought it and sent it to her. She, in turn, did something quite unusual for her. When *Rooster Cogburn* was sold to television some three years later, she wrote an article for *TV Guide* entitled 'Hooked on John Wayne.' Describing Duke, she wrote, in part:

From head to toe, he's all of a piece. Big head. Wide blue eyes. Sandy hair. Rugged skin—lined by living and fun and character . . . A face alive with humor . . . and a sharp wit. Dangerous when roused. His shoulders are broad—very. His chest massive—very. When I leaned against him (which I did as often as possible I must confess), thrilling. It was like leaning against a great tree . . .

And the base of this incredible creation. A pair of small sensitive feet. Carrying this huge frame as though it was a feather. Light of tread. Springy. Dancing. Pretty feet.

Very observing. Very aware. Ready to laugh. To be laughed at. To answer. To stick his neck out. Funny. Outrageous. Spoiled. Self-indulgent. Tough. Full of charm. Knows it. Uses it. Disregards it . . .

As an actor he has an extraordinary gift. A unique naturalness. A very subtle capacity to think and express and caress the camera—the audience. A secret between them.

When you buy a cotton shirt, you want to get . . . good simple long-lasting cotton. No synthetics. That's what you get when you get John Wayne. That's what I got. And as you can see, I liked it.

That's what I got too—and I loved it.

We went back to California aboard Chick Iverson's private plane, and on the spur of the moment Duke decided we should land in Napa Valley and take a tour of the wine country. We went around all the different wineries, tasted the samples, and ordered several bottles sent home, together with a set of huge wine glasses, each of which held an entire bottle of wine. Duke couldn't resist shopping no matter where we were.

We stayed at the Silverado Hotel on that stop-over—an intoxicating, romantic evening. I remember telling Duke, 'Oh, I could stay here forever. I wish we didn't have to rush home.'

'Oh, I don't know about that,' he replied, mysteriously. 'There's a little surprise for you at Orange County Airport.'

'Surprise? Who in the world can be there?'

But it wasn't a 'who.' It was a 'what.' One more way in which Duke said, 'I love you.'

CHAPTER 7

SHORTLY before we had left for Oregon, Duke noticed that I'd been having difficulties with my 1969 Mustang. The hundred-mile round trip to Newport each day wasn't bothering me, but it was more than the car's little engine could cope with.

One evening, after I had had a terrible time starting it up, I'd said, 'Well, I'll either have to get a new car or make my headquarters in Newport Beach.'

As it turned out, both my wishes were about to come true. When our plane touched down at the Orange County Airport, a beautiful new Mercury Monarch Ghia was in a hangar waiting for me. Duke had seen the automobile on a TV commercial one evening, liked it, and had a friend with a car dealership in Grants Pass, Oregon, order it and have it delivered to Newport. Just like that! An early Christmas present, since I was planning to spend the holidays with my folks in Louisiana.

And Duke had another surprise for me. He owned a little two-bedroomed mobile home on the opposite end of Newport Bay, on Lido Peninsula. He had originally bought it so his masseur, Ralph Volkie, would have a place to stay overnight, but Volkie didn't use it much, and for the most part the mobile home remained unoccupied. Since rentals in Newport were becoming astronomical, Duke thought it would be a dandy idea for me to move to Lido, rent-free, as soon as my lease in Marina Del Rey expired the following March. The place was in total disarray. 'But a thorough cleanup, a paint job, and new drapes and carpeting will make it good as new,' Duke insisted.

And so it was that a few months later I moved into my newly decorated little doll's house on Lido Peninsula. For weeks afterward Duke liked to come by and help with the finishing touches, and sometimes he stayed while I cooked dinner. I loved those evenings the best—just the two of us alone.

It was growing increasingly difficult to keep those evenings to ourselves, however. By now the press was on to the fact that Duke had been seeing me quite a lot. One headline in a supermarket newspaper proclaimed DUKE HAS OPERATION TO SATISFY NEW LOVE! Can you imagine? The story was about the knee surgery Duke had undergone right after returning from *Rooster Cogburn*, to repair the cartilage that had been torn during that raft accident. *To satisfy new love?* Duke had been on a walker for three weeks afterward!

But it was not hard to figure out why the gossip was floating around. There'd been all the lunches and dinners, with his friends and without, and all the traveling around. Just recently Duke had had to go to Australia for business, and decided to mix it with pleasure by detouring through Hong Kong, Singapore, and Japan on the way back. Naturally he had brought me along, and naturally it had not escaped notice. (The highlight of that trip for me was the Imperial Hotel in Tokyo, where they actually registered us as 'Mr and Mrs John Wayne'! It sounded so lovely—and Duke didn't try to correct the error.)

Nevertheless, we were still trying hard not to bring undue attention to ourselves. Duke didn't want our relationship made into a circus, and there was Pilar and the family to think about. Pilar had still not officially filed for divorce, and Duke had been quoted as saying, 'If she finds someone she wants, fine. She can have a divorce anytime she wants one. I like and respect her as a friend. But I imagine we'll stay separated . . . There will be no more marriages for me. I'm sixty-eight goddamn years old. I've got twenty grandchildren, and I've got my work, and I don't have to go chasing around.'

That's what he said publicly, and it was no lie. He didn't have to go chasing around. He had me. Privately, he told me, 'Things would be different, Pat, if I were forty-five, even fifty, years old. There's so many things I want to do for you, and with you, but . . .'

In late March he finally decided 'To hell with the press.' Before we'd left for Australia the Academy's board of governors had voted a special Oscar to seventy-eight-year-old director Howard Hawks and invited Duke to be the official presenter at the March 29 ceremonies. Duke had been delighted to accept. Now he wanted me at his side. Four days before the ceremonies he told me, 'Go into town and pick up the prettiest evening gown you can find. I'm taking you to the Academy Awards Tuesday night and showing you off.'

It killed me to do it, but I refused. I dreaded the publicity, the questions, the flashbulbs. We had a big argument, but I wouldn't change my mind. I had always wanted to go to the Academy Awards and to the ball afterward, and to go as Duke's date would have been something extra special, but I knew I wasn't up to it emotionally. Duke felt my attitude was childish, and maybe it was, but I simply didn't want to go.

We reached a compromise of sorts. Duke had reserved a suite for the night at the Beverly Wilshire Hotel, and I agreed to drive into town with him, watch the show on television, and then have a late supper with him afterward. He wasn't too happy about the arrangement, and neither was I, but at least we'd be together. During the drive in from Newport Beach I began to have second thoughts and to wonder if I'd made an awful mistake, but it was too late to do anything about it. It was pouring rain, the shops were closed, and I couldn't very well appear in street clothes. 'Oh, well,' I consoled myself, 'there'll always be a next time.' But the next time wouldn't be until four years later, and the occasion wouldn't be a happy one.

The rest of the evening was no joy, either. Because Duke hated reading from cue cards, he always memorized his speeches, and he was usually letter perfect. But that night he hailed Howard Hawks as 'a man I've worked with in four pictures'—only it was really five. It wasn't the kind of mistake to bother most people, but Duke was annoyed, and he was irritared, too, that they'd played the theme from *True Grit* for his entrance. 'It was an insult to Howard. He wasn't on that film. Why didn't they play "Red River Valley"? *Red River* was the best damn thing we did together.'

Then, because of the downpour, we didn't even bother to go out for dinner; instead we called room service and after a few drinks retired for the evening and returned to Newport the next morning. So much for the glamour of Oscar night.

Throughout most of the spring and summer, Duke stayed pretty close to home. When the *Goose* wasn't chartered, we spent weekends off Catalina Island, with the kids or Duke's friends usually along. During the week Duke spent most of his working hours in business meetings concerning DECO. Two Japanese firms were building plants to make use of the process, and other companies were planning plants in Greece and South Africa. Duke's letters to Washington, however, brought little or no response. 'Those damn politicians won't even send anyone to check out the process,' Duke complained bitterly. 'We developed this for the American people, and foreign countries are the only ones using it.' Finally a couple of men did show up to discuss it, but from their conversation I got the decided feeling that they came to meet John Wayne and didn't really give a damn about processing oil from old rubber tires. Before they left, they made a point of asking for autographed pictures—for their kids. By now, incidentally, Duke had added two new girls, Kathy Milhalovich and Julie Comstock, to the secretarial staff, to assist with the fan mail. His social and business correspondence had become almost a full-time job for me.

Three major events stand out for me that fall. The first was the visit of Emperor Hirohito to Los Angeles. It was to be a one-day whirlwind visit on October 8, and Governor Jerry Brown and Mayor Tom Bradley were hosting a gala banquet for him at the Music Center. They also asked the seventy-four-year-old emperor if there was anything in particular he wanted to see, and he had two personal requests: to visit Disneyland and to meet John Wayne. Duke attended the banquet (a single invitation), and when he returned home he told me he had been seated so far from the VIP tables he had almost been tempted to leave. The city and state officials had commandeered all the better tables for themselves. This had obviously upset Hirohito even more, because he had made a point of asking where Duke was, and then asked to be escorted to his table for the sought-after introduction—much to the embarrassment of those city and state officials. 'I was almost tempted to ask if he had seen any of my old war movies,' Duke said, and laughed. 'Between them all, I must have killed off the entire Japanese army!'

The second event was the annual bull sale at Duke's 26-Bar Ranch, in Stanfield, Arizona. It was held every Thanksgiving and always attracted the most affluent cattle dealers and ranchers throughout the country—though more often than not it was Duke who was the major attraction of the weekend.

Duke had a passion for his Arizona ranch, but because of his frenetic schedule, he couldn't get to Stanfield as often as he wished. He had great confidence in Louis Johnson, though, who kept the place running smoothly and profitably. 'Louie's no bullshit artist,' he would say, to my groans. Duke was obsessive about attending that annual Thanksgiving sale, though, so much so that he insisted on a clause in all his movie contracts guaranteeing he'd be allowed time off to fly to Stanfield in late November, no matter what.

Since Duke had no acting commitments at the time, he decided to pack his Pontiac station wagon and drive, rather than fly, to Stanfield, which is halfway between Tucson and Phoenix. I was none too keen about the trip, not because I had anything against bull sales but because the idea of driving all the way to Arizona with Duke made my blood run cold. The only way I can describe Duke's driving is to say that when he got behind a wheel, he turned into a madman. And that was sober: he never drove when he was drinking. I used to tease him by saying that the patrol cars in Newport raced for the hills when they saw his station wagon approaching. The car was easily identifiable: because of his height, he had had a custom-built top put on so he'd have enough head room.

On the freeways Duke would cut in and out of every lane, from one side to another. Even when he had to turn right out of the left-hand lane, he managed to get across the entire freeway to make that turn. Every other car on the freeway became the 'enemy.' It was frightening. I tried not to nag Duke about it, but one afternoon, when he was in a particularly wild mood, I had to tell him, 'Duke, if anything happens, if you so much as dent another guy's bumper, you know it'll be splashed over every front page in the country tomorrow morning.'

'Come on, Pat, nothing's going to happen,' he said, and it never seemed to.

Well, his luck with the law ran out when we were in Arizona for the bull sale. We didn't dent anyone's bumper, thank God, but we were on an empty road, not another car in sight, and Duke was breaking every speed limit imaginable, when from out of nowhere a big, burly motorcycle cop appeared and maneuvered him to the side of the road.

'And just who do you think you are?' snarled the cop, as if he didn't know. 'Let's have your license.' Duke complied. It was quite obvious that he wasn't going to get out of this one. The cop chewed him out but good, handed him the ticket—and, no, he didn't ask for an autograph. Duke paid the fine, but there was no permanent cure for his insanity once he got behind the steering wheel of that Pontiac.

When we finally got to Stanfield, we had a wonderful Thanksgiving weekend. The ranch was simply lovely. In all, Duke and Louis Johnson owned about seventeen thousand acres, as well as a cattle feedlot that held about eighty-thousand-head capacity. They also owned acreage farther north, in Springerville, which I never saw but which Duke told me was one of the most beautiful places in the world. I could certainly believe it, if the 26-Bar was any indication.

We stayed with the Johnsons that weekend. Alice Johnson prepared a Thanksgiving dinner that rivaled any I had ever eaten; Duke thought her pies were the best he'd ever had, and his attempt at dieting went right out of the window. (Duke had been picking up a lot of excess poundage lately, and he'd been making sporadic, halfhearted attempts to cut down.) Although there were a great many horses available, Duke and I didn't go horseback riding together; during the years I was with him, he never rode a horse except when he was working on a film. After years in the saddle, he obviously didn't consider the activity recreational.

Christmas presented yet another roadblock to his diet, and my fondest memory of all for that winter.

Duke was a very predictable man, a methodical planner, particularly at holiday times. On Halloween he always held an 'open patio' for the kids trick-or-treating; Thanksgiving was always at Stanfield; Christmas, at Bayshore Drive. Duke would pull out all the stops at Christmas: the most beautiful tree, extravagantly trimmed, and dozens of gorgeously wrapped presents beneath the tree for friends and family. He was never bothered by last-minute shopping. Whatever he didn't buy on his trips had been ordered from his beloved catalogues throughout the year.

Up to that year I had always gone home for Christmas, but a few days after Duke and I returned from Stanfield he suggested I call my folks and tell them not to expect me home for the holidays: he wanted me to spend Christmas with him. There was no argument from me. I was thrilled at the prospect.

A few weeks later Duke picked out a magnificent tree and had it delivered to the house. I was all set to unpack the ornaments when he said, 'To hell with it. I'd like to spend the holidays on the *Goose* with you and the kids.'

'But what will we do with the tree?'

'We'll take it along. We can buy ornaments when we get to Mazatlán.'

By the time we *got* to Mazatlán, our tree was a sorry sight, all dried out and half the needles missing, and we had to rush to shore to find another little one and some ornaments—not the easiest things to find in that small community at the last moment. But it didn't matter. The *Goose* itself was a floating Christmas, lights strung from prow to stern. 'Lit up more than old Duke,' he commented.

In addition to Aissa, Ethan, and Marisa, the Iversons were along on the cruise, and it was total-relaxation time. How I loved it, just lying on the upper deck, reading, working on my tan. Duke would get irritated because I could stay in the sun all day and never get burned, whereas he burned rather easily, and because he never wore his hairpiece on the *Goose*, his head turned blushing red, almost as if it were embarrassed to have been caught exposed. We had two ski boats on board, and the kids kept themselves occupied by water-skiing and swimming, or wandering into the salon and joining the card games that were usually in progress.

We toasted the New Year 1976 in Manzanillo harbor and flew back to Newport on Friday, January 2. I was the happiest lady in the world, the luckiest, the most secure. I was looking forward to 1976. Duke was in a wonderful mood because he had another movie on the horizon, and because he felt, as I did, that Marisa, Ethan, and Aissa had accepted me as a member of the family. Apart from a few minor arguments now and again, my relationship with Duke seemed disaster-proof.

On the night of our return, I remember thinking, good heavens, how time flies. Duke and I have been together for nearly three and a half years and it seems like three and a half months.

How could I have predicted that we had reached what would be the halfway point in the time allotted us, by whatever power it is that decides such things. How grateful I am that I *didn't* know that in another three and a half years, all that would remain would be the memories.

Part II
Point of No Return

CHAPTER 8

ON January 8, 1976, we left for Carson City, Nevada, to begin work on Duke's new film, *The Shootist*, the story of an aging gunfighter dying of cancer. The role struck a little closer to home than I would have liked, but Duke was immensely excited about it. 'I have a special understanding of it, don't you see?' he said. 'I belong to a very exclusive club, Pat. Not many of us have recovered from cancer.'

He also thought the story itself, based on a novel by Glendon Swarthout, was great. It wasn't just a shoot-'em-up, though the end of the movie was to be a duel. Instead, there was a lesson to it. When the gunfighter, J. B. Books, is told he has cancer, the discovery mellows him. He loses his arrogance and starts to look differently at the people around him, including a somewhat delinquent boy played by Ron Howard. As Duke said later in an interview, 'In portraying an aging and dying gunfighter, I try to show a young fellow who might have turned out wild that it's not worth it. That's the basic idea of the story, so there is a little bit of moral value. It's about a fellow who has a little more good than bad in him. That's the kind of character I like to play.'

The script had a few problems in it, but Duke soon got those ironed out. One scene called for him to take his pants down as he was being examined by a doctor, and he said no, thank you: 'There aren't going to be any bare asses in any movie I'm in, particularly if the bare ass is mine.' He got to keep his pants on. Also, the original script had the Ron Howard character still 'bad' at the end, and Duke objected strenuously. A few revisions later, the boy, now aware of the futility of violence, had matured. That was a more logical conclusion, to Duke's way of thinking.

As was Duke's custom, we arrived at the location site a few days before the picture was scheduled to go into production. In this way Duke could acclimate himself to the surroundings, meet the townspeople, and get them used to the idea that John Wayne was in town.

He'd have breakfast in a busy coffee shop, talk to everyone who came over, sign autographs, observe all the amenities. He was aware that when visitors came over to him between takes, when his mind was on what he was required to do next, he was apt to be brusque. He just couldn't be interrupted while working. Therefore, if someone who tried to approach him on the set was brushed off and went around saying how nasty John Wayne was, he'd find a lot of people saying, 'Well, he was sure nice to me.' Duke could shrug off public opinion about his politics, but he was insistent about not insulting his fans.

Duke had a large suite in our hotel in Carson City, and I had a single room with twin beds right across the hall. On one of our first nights there, Duke was tired and decided to have dinner for the two of us sent to his room, after which he would go straight to sleep. We hadn't quite finished when a young man came to the door to pick up the dishes. Obviously he had been told only the room number and not the identity of the occupant. Duke had grown a mustache for the role, was in his robe and pajamas, and had shed his hairpiece for the night, so he didn't look at all like the John Wayne people expect. I had all I could do not to laugh when the boy asked, 'Say, do you people know that John Wayne is staying at this hotel?'

Duke replied, without bothering to disguise his voice, 'I heard that. I heard he was here someplace.'

The fellow responded, 'Oh, gosh, I sure would like to

meet him someday.'

'Yeah, that would be nice,' Duke said. 'I'd like to meet him myself!'

The busboy removed the dishes and went on his way. I wonder if anyone ever told him he'd been sent to Duke's room. Duke wasn't being ornery, by the way—just a little vain about being caught with his hairpiece off.

On Tuesday, January 13, *The Shootist* began, and, as usual, Duke began trying to direct his director—in this case, Don Siegel. There were arguments, conferences, compromises: it was the *Rooster Cogburn* story all over again. I didn't help matters, either. On the set I was supposed to be Miss Efficiency, always on hand to bring Duke anything he needed, to take notes, to have his script ready. That was my job, after all, and I loved every bit of it.

This time, however, Miss Efficiency had forgotten to pack Duke's guns. Of course, Paramount's prop department had an entire arsenal of weapons on hand, including 'stand-in' fakes for Duke's guns, but nothing would do but that he have his own guns, which meant calling someone at home and having them flown north posthaste. Luckily my friend Peggy Reagan was free, and Duke agreed that if she brought the guns, she could join us on location for a while: there was always that extra twin bed in my room.

Duke had his guns the following morning, and for the rest of the week everything seemed to go quite well. It was hard for me to be objective about Duke's work, seeing it done in bits and pieces, but even this early it seemed to me some of the best work he'd ever done. Even the arguments between Duke and Don Siegel seemed to simmer down. And then, quite suddenly, everything fell apart—or so I thought.

Duke wasn't in a very good mood on Monday the 19th; the location shooting was beginning to get to him again. The change of weather and altitude and the excess weight he was carrying were aggravating his breathing problem. Peggy and I decided to cheer him up. We'd really fix ourselves up for dinner in Duke's room that night, and, since Peggy was going home the next day, it'd be a little farewell party.

When we presented ourselves at the door to his suite that evening, instead of the compliment I'd been hoping for, I got, 'Why are you so dressed up? Where are you going?'

'Nowhere.'

'Oh, yes, you are. You two are preparing to go out to dinner by yourselves somewhere. You knew I wasn't feeling so red-hot today and I wanted to eat in my room.'

Of course I did. I told him so and swore that Peggy and I expected to eat in his suite with him, and that we had dressed up only because we wanted to make the evening a little festive, and cheer him up, but—

'Like hell you did!' he replied angrily. He pulled off the cap he had been wearing in lieu of his hairpiece and threw it at me, shouting, 'Just get out of here.'

By that time I had had just about enough. It was bad enough that Duke was accusing me of something I had no intention of doing, but worse was the fact that he refused to believe I was telling the truth.

'Come on, Peggy, let's go,' I said.

Once downstairs, we ran into some old friends who happened to be vacationing at the hotel, and they invited us to join them for dinner. I told Peggy to go ahead and join them. I was just too damn mad to eat.

I wandered into the casino, found a seat at the blackjack table, ordered a drink, and started playing as if my life depended on the turn of the cards. And I started winning. With each new drink I ordered, the more recklessly I played, and the better time I had. After a while I left the blackjack table to play craps, and I didn't lose there, either. By the time Peggy dragged me back, bleary-eyed, to my room, I had won over six hundred dollars. I had just enough strength left to leave a wake-up call for five A.M. and verify that

Duke had left one for the same hour, and then I went to sleep. After all, I still had a job. I thought.

At five-thirty I was in Duke's room to help him get his stuff together for the day's work. I offered no explanation of where I'd gone the night before, and since I had one of life's super hangovers, I was in no mood for an argument. He was, however. He picked up the quarrel where we had left off the night before—'How *could* you? You know I'm sick'—and I decided to say nothing, nothing at all, as I got his wardrobe, hairpiece, cap, and other paraphernalia neatly packed. The quieter I remained, the angrier he got. Finally he shouted at me, 'You're fired!'

I opened my mouth—but what could I say? Duke was obviously in no mood to listen to reason, and I wasn't feeling very reasonable myself. Was this it, I wondered? The end of Miss Stacy and boss man Wayne. What about Pat and Duke? It was crazy, but I just kept quiet.

Duke was the first to break the silence.

'You can stay on working for me here while you're out looking for another job.' And what did he expect me to do here in Carson City, Nevada? Play blackjack for the house? That struck me as terribly funny, but I didn't smile.

Obviously aware of my hung-over condition, he continued in an equally gruff manner, 'Get yourself some coffee and have one of the studio drivers bring you to the set in an hour. And remember—you're fired!'

Off he went. Now what was I supposed to do? I decided to follow his advice and get some coffee, and then just to play it cool once I was on the set. I'd do my job as usual and hope no one would notice anything was wrong.

Gossip travels fast on location. By the time I'd got to the set, it seemed everyone knew about my lucky streak the night before—not only knew but had to comment about it to Duke. 'God, I wish I could play that game like your secretary,' I heard one of them say.

I groaned. Things were bad enough between us. I was sure this kind of thing could only make things worse.

Duke finished his main scene for the morning and, as usual, retreated inside the motor home. I walked around outside, freezing and miserable. Then I heard the door open; he put his arms around me and said, 'Come on, get in here where it's warm.'

Once inside, he said, 'Hey, I heard you did okay last night. How much did you take them for?'

'Oh, over six hundred dollars'.

'Good for you.' He laughed. 'Don't spend it all in one place.'

And that was it. My period of unemployment had lasted about half a day. Duke never mentioned firing me again, and I knew better than to kid him about it. It was better to leave well enough alone.

There were other periods over the next couple of years, however, when I would be sorely tempted to quit: times after an argument when I'd feel I couldn't put up with things the way they were. After a while, though, Duke would always ask, 'What's bugging you?' And I'd reply, 'Well, you did this or said such and such, and made me feel about ten inches tall.'

His usual response would be, 'But, honey, why didn't you tell me?' and my usual reply would be, 'I did, but you were shouting so loud you couldn't hear me.' And, just as in Carson City, everything would be fine again.

Another small incident helped make up for that night, as far as Duke was concerned. A few nights after my triumph at the gaming tables, he decided we should both go downstairs to the casino and win a bundle. He deposited me at the blackjack table, 'since everyone tells me you can't do anything wrong,' he said, and went off to play some craps. Needless to say, craps suddenly became the only game in town, and the crowds became so impossible he finally just had to give up on it and make a graceful exit. So graceful, in fact, that for fifteen minutes or so I wasn't even aware he had gone to his room. I hurried upstairs to see if everything was all right, and asked why he didn't come by my table and get me.

'Didn't want to break in on your game. How much did you get them for tonight?'

'Five dollars.'

'Good. Now let's play some backgammon for cash.'

Duke always said that when somebody else won, it was luck, but when he won, it was skill. He was very skillful that night. I left the room minus that five dollars. You can't win them all, and in this case, I think I may have won by losing.

Duke's night at the crap table was something of an exception for him. He did very little socializing after hours while on location for *The Shootist*—because of his health. Most nights, he was so tired all he wanted to do was have an early dinner, maybe play some cards, and go to bed. He didn't even have dinner with his co-stars as much as he had on *Rooster Cogburn*, even though he liked them all—Jimmy Stewart, Lauren Bacall, Ron Howard.

Ron was the only one he saw much of, as a matter of fact. Duke considered Ron one of the finest young actors he'd ever worked with, and there was great mutual admiration between them. Duke never made it appear as if he was trying to direct Ron or tell him what to do. Instead he'd gently ask, 'What do you think about trying the scene this way?' 'How do you feel about that?' Ron came pretty close to stealing the film, which was just fine with Duke. The two of them had a special empathy, which I think comes over in the film.

One of the few exceptions Duke did make to his staying-in habit was to help out an old friend. Ronald Reagan had a huge fund raiser coming up to boost his campaign for the 1976 Republican presidential nomination, and because of his work schedule and health, Duke had at first sent regrets. But Paul Laxalt, the Republican senator from Nevada and one of Reagan's right-hand men, had persuaded him to change his mind, and so when Duke wasn't working on his lines, he was working on the speech he planned to deliver.

When the night came, we worked all day on *The Shootist* and rushed back to the hotel; then we dressed and sped to the fund raiser. We arrived shortly after seven P.M. Neither Laxalt nor anyone from his staff was on hand to greet Duke or take him to the podium. Most of the guests by then were quite intoxicated. Duke was really steamed, because after such a big deal had been made about how important it was for him to be there, he was now being totally ignored. Even when some assistant finally brought him to the platform and he started into his speech, no one seemed to be paying much attention. He had a few choice words to say about that evening later, I can tell you.

Another selection of choice words came after another official function, though this time it wasn't the function itself that was at fault.

On January 23 location shooting for *The Shootist* finally finished at Carson City, and the whole movie was moved to the Warner Brothers studio lot in Burbank, which had been leased by Paramount for the duration of the filming. Paramount had rented two apartments, again across the hall from each other, at the nearby Oakwood Gardens, which was to be our temporary home until the picture was completed.

Duke's cook, Fausto, lived a few towns away in Encino, so it was easy for him to come by in the early afternoon, cook dinner in my apartment, wash the dishes, and then return home early. He was delighted, since his long drive to work in Newport had been shortened to ten minutes. Most of the 'living' was done in my apartment; Duke used his for business appointments. It was a wild arrangement, but great fun.

It got even wilder a week later, when Duke took me to a black-tie affair at the Beverly Hilton Hotel for Prime Minister Itzhak Rabin, of Israel.

The evening itself was just lovely, and Duke as usual made a point of seeing that I was not ignored. No matter who came over, he'd say, 'I'd like you to meet Miss Stacy.' Not 'my secretary' or 'Pat'—always 'Miss Stacy.' During those social evenings I was his *lady*, and had I been Grace Kelly, he'd have acted no differently.

That evening, there were a great number of photographers around, and one of their pictures found its way into the pages of another one of those supermarket tabloids. I was lying in bed with the flu one morning when Duke came storming into my room at the Oakwood Gardens, threw the newspaper on my bed, and let loose with a stream of expletives.

I looked at the paper. JOHN WAYNE 'MADLY IN LOVE' WITH HIS SECRETARY, ran the headline. 'She's the only girl for me,' reveals John Wayne . . . and Pat admits, 'I'm *his* girl—and he's *my* man . . .'

'These bastards say you talked to them. Did you do that?'

'Of course not, Duke. They called me up, but I told them I had nothing to say. You know I'd never do that.'

'Are you sure? They made this stuff all up?'

'Yes, yes, of course. You know what they're like.'

I looked at the front page again, and I couldn't stop myself from smiling.

'What are you so pleased about?'

'Well,' I replied, 'it's an awfully good picture of me, and I'm referred to as the "twenty-four-year-old Pat Stacy." I was then thirty-four and a half.

That was the wrong thing to say.

'Well, it's a lousy picture of me, and I come out of it looking like a dirty old man. Now you get busy and write these bastards. Tell them I'm going to sue their asses off unless they do something about this story.'

I dashed off a letter threatening mayhem unless they printed an apology and admitted that I never gave them an interview, but nothing ever came of it.

Eventually Duke dropped it. It seemed that everyone connected with *The Shootist* had seen that front page, however, and I was in for my share of teasing that day. The article also opened the door for any number of stories that followed, and no matter how much time passed, I remained the 'twenty-four-year-old Pat Stacy.'

On April 5 Don Siegel called it a wrap on *The Shootist*. We were supposed to have finished several days before, but in mid-March Duke had come down with an ear infection so painful he had had to miss ten days of work. He had hated to do that—he never could stand people who made excuses for not working—so as soon as he could, he had dragged himself back, still in pain, to finish his scenes. When his last scene had been completed, we all breathed a sigh of relief.

Neither Duke nor I had the vaguest premonition that *The Shootist* would be his final movie credit.

A few months later the producer, Mike Frankovich, brought a rough cut of *The Shootist* to the house. The Gordeans drove down to see it as well, and Aissa, Ethan, and Marisa joined us for the evening.

Whenever Duke had a private screening, whether of one of his films or one of somebody else's, he also provided a running commentary as the film progressed, on everything from performance to sets, photography, and technical details. This time Duke was pleased with both the movie and his performance in it. However, what I remember most vividly about that evening was Marisa's reaction to the film. Her face was streaked with tears when the lights came on, and she couldn't stop crying in spite of all our efforts to calm her. I don't know if Marisa had seen any of the other movies in which Duke's character died, but this one was different. She saw her dad dying of cancer. Although Marisa had been born two years after Duke had had his lung removed, she was still very aware of what it meant.

Finally, Ethan had to tell her, 'Stop acting so silly.

95

It's only a movie. Dad is sitting right here next to you.'

But it was several minutes more before she could stop.

CHAPTER 9

AFTER three months of back-breaking work on *The Shootist* and his siege of illness, all Duke wanted after filming the movie was a spell of rest and relaxation aboard the *Wild Goose*, and during that spring and summer I think the happiest times we ever spent were aboard that boat.

Not that Duke took it easy during the next several months. We always seemed to be dashing somewhere: to Chicago for a Notre Dame Club award and a Boys' Club fund raiser; to Philadelphia for a dinner in honor of Queen Elizabeth (what a thrill that was!); to Wyoming to lead a Fourth of July parade; to just about everywhere to promote *The Shootist*, which Paramount was rushing out in July.

Duke was disappointed and angry that Paramount was doing that. He felt that the subject was hardly light summer entertainment and needed a much more thoughtful publicity campaign. 'Those people are putting all their damn time into *King Kong*. They think the Wayne movie will make it on its own. Well, it won't. People don't go to see a movie just because my name is on the marquee. Those bastards don't understand that. It used to be the case, but it's not the case anymore.'

Whenever he could, though, he returned to the *Wild Goose*, and we'd go sailing blissfuly apart from the rest of the world, down to Mexico or up to northwest Washington to fish for salmon. Sometimes Duke would invite some of his friends along; other times, Ethan, Aissa, or Marisa would be aboard; but the times I treasured most were when it was just the two of us, rocking on the blue waters or exploring the towns along the shore. No business, no responsibilities, just lost in our own private world.

When Duke finished *The Shootist*, we joined the *Wild Goose* in Acapulco, and for the next two weeks we sailed up the coast to Puerto Vallarta. We'd swim off the big boat in warm Mexican waters, lie side by side on the deck, soaking in the sun, or take the little boat to shore and just wander around and shop. Duke could never resist a shop, and by the end of the trip he'd bought me enough Mexican blouses to open my own store. In the evenings we'd play cards, read a little, kiss.

There was a marked improvement in Duke's health. The breathing problems hadn't disappeared entirely, but it wasn't as bad as before, and I couldn't help wondering if it wouldn't be a good idea for Duke to take it easy more often, cut down on the public schedule, even on the movies. He'd already done everything. Why did he have to keep driving himself so? What more did he want?

I asked him that question one evening, and I'll never forget his answer. 'Pat,' he said, 'you've got to understand something. As long as a man has a project—*something* to look forward to—there'll always be something important to him. He'll never really get old. If I had nothing to look forward to, I might as well be dead.' Then he smiled. 'You know hard work never killed anyone.'

'Are you trying to get me to work harder?' I teased.

'No, a man couldn't ask for a more dedicated slave.'

Then he was silent for a few minutes. Finally he said, 'But you can't turn back the clock. I'll be sixty-nine this year, Pat, sixty-nine goddamned years. There's no such thing as growing old gracefully. It's all deterioration, decay. You just can't give in to it.' He looked at me and then looked down. 'You should remember that. You know, I've heard that the same day a newspaper

98

announces the wedding of some guy over sixty-five to a young woman, its editors start preparing his obituary. I'm thirty-four years older than you.'

'But, Duke,' I protested, 'I told you a thousand times, the difference in our ages doesn't matter to me. I never even think about it.'

'But I do,' he replied. 'Often. And *you* will, ten years from now.'

I hushed him up, but I know it was something that continued to prey on his mind. His seventh decade was drawing to a close, and he was mad as hell about it; jealous of younger men, jealous, I often thought, of his sons, and even of me. But he wouldn't give in to it.

With the coming of fall, Duke only stepped up his schedule all the more. It was as if he were driven to pack in as much activity as he could, to make every week count. Socially, it was a rare evening when two to a half-dozen people weren't over to the house, and professionally Duke was all over the place, taping segments for a Lucille Ball special, a Rodgers and Hammerstein special, NBC's *The Big Event*. The latter was to promote *The Shootist*, which was indeed meeting the fate that Duke had predicted: vacation time was simply not the time to release a picture about a man dying of cancer. In spite of good reviews, *The Shootist* was floundering at the box office, and Duke was as deeply troubled about that as he was over the fact that he hadn't received a good new script all year. *The Shootist* meant something to Duke, and he was determined to see that it was kept alive, even if he had to do it single-handedly. Besides, there was talk in the air that the picture might land Duke a third Oscar nomination. Although we never talked about it, I knew he wanted it—wanted it for the picture and wanted it for himself. He simply wasn't sure how many more quality starring roles he could find for a man his age.

I remember one script sent to him, intended as a co-starring vehicle for him and Clint Eastwood, and

Duke's disgust when he told me, 'This kind of stuff is all they know how to write these days: the sheriff is the heavy, the townspeople a bunch of jerks; someone like me and Eastwood ride into town, know everything, act the big guys, and everyone else is a bunch of idiots.' Since the script was still untitled when Duke received it, I have no idea if it was ever produced, but Duke didn't like that kind of story line. 'I'm interested in the basic emotions,' he told me. 'A kid's love, a woman's love, a man's love.'

Of all the television specials he did that fall, there was one that was truly special. The Variety Clubs International, a show-business charitable organization Duke had long supported, wanted to raise funds for a new cancer wing on a children's hospital in Miami, and several months before, they had approached Duke with the idea of staging an 'all-star tribute to John Wayne.' Duke had readily agreed, and after a great many conferences and planning sessions, it finally happened.

It was a black-tie affair, taped for ABC on a huge soundstage at Warner Brothers' Burbank studios on Saturday night, November 6, for a November 26 airing. Producer Paul Keyes had done a marvelous job lining up people to pay tribute to Duke: co-stars such as Maureen O'Hara, Claire Trevor Bren, Glen Campbell, Lee Marvin, James Stewart, Angie Dickinson, and Ron Howard. Bob Hope would tell jokes, and Frank Sinatra would host the entire testimonial and sing a few songs personally dedicated to Duke.

Duke and his family were placed at a table for twelve in the center of the barnlike room. We had had a couple of discussions about whether I should be at the table, too, but both Duke and I felt it would be better if it were just the family, so it was Duke, Aissa, Marisa, and Ethan; Duke's older daughters, Melinda, and Toni, and their husbands; and Patrick and Michael Wayne and their wives.

Frank Sinatra sang 'You Are the Sunshine of My Life.' Claire Trevor made a simple, sincere speech paying tribute to Duke, calling him 'one of the world's greatest stars and my dearest friend.' Maureen O'Hara, looking gorgeous and vibrant, sang 'I've Grown Accustomed to *His* Face,' recalling the five pictures in which they'd co-starred. Then she descended the stairs from the stage; Duke rose to his feet, kissed each of her delicate hands, and stood alongside her as she finished the song. There wasn't a dry eye in the house.

If that was a highlight of the evening, Charles Bronson's tribute to macho had to be the low point. It was obvious that no one had bothered to ask Duke his feelings on the subject. Bronson said, 'Macho is John Wayne and has been for fifty years,' but he was wrong. Duke had always felt that the word meant an exaggerated masculine pride, something phony that drew attention to itself by struts and poses. Real masculinity, he felt, was something innate; it made itself felt through action and quiet resolve rather than through ostentation. Everybody knows the saying, 'A man's got to do what a man's got to do': it's become a part of the standard Wayne imitation. Yet that really *was* the essence of Duke. Macho was for those who felt they had something to prove. Duke had nothing to prove. 'Christ, how I hate that word!' he said.

The best joke of the evening, and there were many, came when Frank Sinatra 'officially' introduced Duke to the audience in order to present him with a bronze statue, and Duke made his entrance by walking through a specially constructed stage wall. But it was really his thank-you speech that had the audience—and me—emotional.

Tonight you made an old man and an actor very happy. (You are happy, aren't you Frank?) . . . Folks, the show got ahead of me. I tried to write down some things when you were all talking, but I can't . . . When you get to be my age, you let a lot of people get away from you that you wish you could thank . . . I don't know. Who ever thought

101

that Molly Morrison's kid would end up being done in bronze? ... I wish I had the time and energy to thank each one of you. I sure liked where I sat, and I loved everyone at that table. They're all great kids, all healthy, thank God. There are a lot of kids who haven't been that fortunate all over the world. That's why we're here tonight—to help young kids. I've been proud of having my name on marquees around the world, but I'm prouder knowing that it will be on a wing of a children's hospital for the Variety Clubs. And to all you folks out there, I want to thank you for these last fifty years of my career. And I hope I can keep at it for another fifty years—or at least until I can get it right. Thank you.

Afterward, at dinner, he turned to me and said, laughingly, 'I hope those people out there didn't think that was my eulogy.'

CHAPTER 10

ON December 2 Duke went into Hoag Hospital for surgery. It wasn't anything serious, just some corrective surgery on the prostate gland, but I couldn't help worrying nonetheless. I knew it wasn't uncommon to uncover cancer of the prostate during such operations, and Duke wasn't in the best of shape. Fortunately, nothing dire was discovered, and after a few days of rest and tests, Duke was allowed to go home.

If only his doctor and I had had that little trouble getting Duke *into* the hospital! Duke's condition had been diagnosed weeks before, but he wouldn't hear of going into surgery until all his current commitments had been met, and he had quite a list of them. Besides all his television projects, he was about to embark on a first-time-ever experience for him: making a commercial.

Over the next couple of years he'd received hundreds of letters about those commercials, people writing in from all over to express disappointment, to wonder why he had 'lowered himself' to become a television salesman. His answer to them all was terse and truthful: 'I did it for the M-U-N-Y. But I guess I made a mistake. I'll just have to find another way.'

Actually, he realized he had made a mistake long before the first commercial was even aired. The entire experience was a nightmare.

The Bristol Myers Company had a new aspirin-substitute product it wanted to launch, called Datril 500. Since it had to compete with Tylenol, the effectiveness of its advertising would be crucial, and the company wanted a spokesman whose very presence emanated trust and confidence: Duke. Duke was not for it, at first, but he did need money, and the pharmaceutical giant ultimately came up with an offer Duke simply could not afford to refuse: six figures for two short series of commercials, as well as an agreement to respect any suggestions Duke might have that would be beneficial to the commercials.

That sounded great, and, in fact, Duke's first suggestion was received enthusiastically. Why not shoot the first series of commercials in Monument Valley?

Monument Valley, of course, is as familiar to viewers of John Ford Westerns as the Empire State Building is to *King Kong* buffs. In fact, it was because of such films as *Stagecoach, Fort Apache, She Wore a Yellow Ribbon,* and *The Searchers* that it became emblematic of the American West. If there is such a thing as God's country, this is it: a world unto itself, encompassing two thousand square miles in northeast Arizona and southeast Utah and dominated by the huge, glove-shaped rock formations called the Mittens.

Monument Valley first became famous when John Ford used it as a location for *Stagecoach,* but according to Duke, it was *he,* not Ford, who originally found the place. He had been hired as an assistant for a George O'Brien Western, and one of his jobs had been to get 400 head of cattle into a canyon 150 miles from any paved road. In gathering them, he had ridden into Monument Valley. In a letter to the *Saturday Evening Post* in 1979, Duke wrote:

For ten years I held that back as a possible future location. Finally when John Ford decided to use me for a lead in *Stagecoach,* he said, 'Now if I could only find a fresh picturesque area to represent the West of the 1800s.' I promptly suggested Monument Valley. He promptly suggested that I was hired as the actor and not as the director; but he took note of what I had said and upon his return from location hunting, I was standing with some of the crew when he approached, and said, 'I have found the most colourful location that can ever be used for a picture.' Then he looked directly at me and said, 'Monument Valley.' And I assure you from that moment on, Jack Ford discovered Monument Valley.

Duke was delighted at the prospect of showing me the valley, one of his 'favourite places in the world.' I was equally thrilled. He had talked about it so much that I could hardly wait to see it for myself. And indeed my first glimpse of the place was everything that had been promised: the endless expanse of red-gold earth, the pure blue sky, the towering Mittens.

The delight soon wore off, however, as the shooting began. First of all, Duke was incensed by what he considered the crew's total disregard for the proper lighting and camera work, so important to capture the magnificence of the valley. Since Duke had made several movies there, he knew exactly what was needed, but nobody paid any attention, and endless hours were wasted. I remember his saying to me, 'Pappy knew what he was doing. He got the shadows when he needed them. Those monuments and this valley worked for him.' (And he wasn't wrong. When the commercial was finally aired, Duke's gardener protested—and I swear these are her words—'Why did they have to use that phony-looking background?')

On top of that there were constant arguments about what would and would not go into the script. To give just one example, when filming at a second location north of Flagstaff, Duke wanted a reference to the magnificent aspen trees in the background, and the ad people almost went into cardiac arrest. 'Aspen' sounded too much like 'aspirin'! And so it went.

Things got so bad that Duke even made up a joke about it. 'The next commercial, this is what we'll have. We'll do a commercial about the making of a commercial; we'll show the meetings, the discussions with attorneys and ad executives, all the chaos I went through. And then I'll step before the cameras and say, "This really gives you a headache. Take Datril 500. It's strong medicine!" '

It was a great private joke, but, God, Duke was frustrated. He was a professional, however, and insisted on giving his best performance take after take. He never tried to walk through the part. He was in Monument Valley and intended to work just as hard as he had on every movie he had made there.

Although I have made references to Duke's refusal to live in the past, during the time we were on that location, he *was* back in the past; there was no way of avoiding it. I recall one lunch hour when he took me on a private tour of the area where much of *Stagecoach* had been filmed, and from his conversation I realized just how much he missed John Ford and all his old buddies: the high jinks, the hard work, the camaraderie. 'All gone,' he said sadly. 'Never to return. That was yesterday; nothing remains the same.'

Finally, it was over. Duke had another series of Datril 500 commericals to film the following April, and I was sure that after this experience there wouldn't be enough money in the United States Treasury to persuade him to do another. (As it turned out, I was wrong. The Great Western Savings and Loan Company made a series of local commercials with Duke that fall, and they turned out to be a dream: Duke in Grants Pass, Oregon, talking about the American West and, of course, about Great Western. He even got Ethan and Marisa in the commercial, cuddled in sleeping bags in the background.)

With the Datril 500 commercials finished, it was off the next day for the annual bull sale at Stanfield, and then *finally* into Hoag Hospital for the prostate surgery. In a way, actually, the prostate surgery was a blessing in disguise. Duke was forced to slow down in spite of himself. For the next whole month he stayed close to home, turning down holiday invitations and taking it easy. And I got to spend my first Christmas at the house.

Nothing in the world could compare with that first Christmas in Newport. During Christmas week there was a special boat parade, all the ships gaily decorated for the season, for which we had a front-row seat from Duke's patio. A great many of the skippers had installed loudspeakers on their ships so they could transmit greetings to the people onshore. Duke had his own speakers and microphone, so he could in turn shout Merry Christmas to the ships as they passed his house. This was as much a part of the Christmas ritual as trimming the tree and passing out presents. And if some friend came by unexpectedly, Duke made sure he didn't go home empty-handed. There were extra gifts for all such emergencies.

Throughout Christmas week the house was filled with friends and family, people coming and going all the time for cocktails and dinner. The younger children were with us, and the older ones came and went in shifts, bringing their children with them, staying awhile, then leaving to visit other members of their families. Duke talked of holding a massive family reunion, but I don't think he was up to it. On Christmas day I wore a green velvet skirt, the same as I'd bought Marisa the week before for a party she was going to. Duke loved that—the two of us dressed almost identically.

On New Year's Eve it was just the two of us, alone. We kissed and toasted one another at the stroke of midnight, and quietly reaffirmed our love.

The following day Duke had his traditional New Year's Day bash at the house: a lot of Duke's friends and all the younger children. The women spent the day in the kitchen while the men played cards and watched the football games. The only thing that made this New Year's Day stand out was the fact that I came close to burning Duke's house to the ground.

Duke's cook had the day off, and the other women and I were in the kitchen, cooking and drinking champagne. There were two ovens in the kitchen, and we were using both, since we had so many things going. Suddenly smoke and flames started pouring out of one of them. I shut off the stove and opened the oven door, and an enormous blaze burst out at me. In the excitement I couldn't find the fire extinguisher, which was right on the wall, and so grabbed some baking soda, which only made matters worse. I called into the living room, 'Joe, will you please come here for a minute,' and when Joe DeFranco was in range, I whispered, 'We're on fire!' In a minute he had found the extinguisher and doused the flames. It seems a skillet of cooking oil had been left in the previously unused oven, and we had forgotten to check before preheating it. Not one of my brighter days! And our problems weren't over yet. Joe poured the oil into the garbage disposal, but since the dishwasher was going at the time, the garbage disposal started backing up into the sink, and we had to get a bucket brigade going out the kitchen door to remove the water from the sink before it could flow over onto the floor. Glenia Reafsnyder found a wrench, and we tried to open an outside pipe, but to no avail. In desperation I recalled our regular plumber, who wasn't particularly thrilled about leaving his football games, but he came over and solved our problems with what seemed disheartening ease.

After he left we cleaned up the mess and got back to the business of preparing dinner. Although he was just a room away, Duke had been totally oblivious of our combined fire and flood. His concentration had been divided between the card game going on and the football games he had been watching simultaneously on three televison sets.

When we broke the news to him at dinner, all he said was, 'Well, thank God you didn't burn the house down.'

All over America people were celebrating the holidays, and some no doubt were envying the glamorous life of celebrities and wondering what wild and romantic things the rich and famous were doing to bring in the new year. Well, that's what we were doing—and they could have it.

CHAPTER 11

BY now Duke was feeling well enough to get up and around, and the result was one of the most incongruous political partnerships in years.

Duke's politics, of course, were well known. He'd always been a conservative and rock-ribbed Republican, and during the campaign he'd worked his tail off, first for Ronald Reagan, then for candidate Ford, even though Gerald Ford had been a distinct second choice in his eyes. That's why he reacted with a whoop of laughter when the invitaion came in the mail: the president's inaugural committee wanted *him* to speak at a grand preinaugural gala in honor of President-elect Jimmy Carter.

'Pat!' he roared. 'Did you see this? What d'you suppose they want me to do? Dress up as a peanut?' He continued in that vein for a few more minutes, but when he was done making jokes, he promptly accepted. His views on candidate Jimmy Carter might have been occasionally unprintable, but it was President-elect Carter now, and Duke had always had the utmost respect for the office. 'Besides,' he said, 'I'll show those so-called liberals I'm not the devil they say I am. And who knows,' he added grinning, 'maybe your Southern buddy will invite us for lunch.' Duke knew I was just as much a Republican as he was, but I had always been somewhat chauvinistically Southern, and Duke teased me about it all the time. From then on, President Carter was periodically referred to as 'your Southern buddy.'

The gala was due to take place at the Kennedy

Center in Washington, D.C., on January 19, and we flew in a day early so Duke could rehearse. He was nursing a bad cold, but he hung around most of the afternoon to do his bit and then turned up early the next day to rehearse the finale with the entire company. Among the others to appear at the gala were Bette Davis, Paul Newman and Joanne Woodward, Shirley MacLaine, Chevy Chase and Dan Aykroyd from *Saturday Night Live*, Leonard Bernstein, Linda Ronstadt, Mike Nichols and Elaine May, Loretta Lynn, Redd Foxx, the Alvin Ailey Dance Company—a real cross-section of the performing arts.

At six P.M., one hour before the scheduled showtime, the cast was still rehearsing *God Bless America*, and still getting it all screwed up. By now everyone was slaphappy. Leonard Bernstein put an arm around Paul Simon as they went into the song for the umpteenth time; then, in the middle of the second chorus, they began to pantomime the raising of the flag, while Bette Davis bellowed brassily. Chevy Chase broke out of line and began doing Ed Sullivan gestures, which inspired Bernstein to break out of line and tap dance, while Elaine May and Mike Nichols couldn't decide whether to put their hands over their hearts or salute.

'I just couldn't believe it,' Duke told me afterward. Nor could he believe Bette Davis taking off her shoes at the reception after the gala and dashing around in stocking feet. 'There's a time and place for everything,' he griped, 'and that wasn't the time or the place, no matter how uncomfortable her shoes were.' He told me it took a lot of willpower to keep him from giving Miss Davis 'one hell of a lecture' on proper etiquette. Can you imagine Duke and Davis in a brawl?

Then the big occasion arrived, and, miraculously, everything came off. With the exception of Duke, Hollywood's leading Republicans were conspicuous by their absence, which gave Duke's appearance a stunning impact. It was almost like one of his movies: the outnumbered individual emerging triumphant.

Even though everything was on cue cards, Duke had memorized his lines, of course, though he hadn't been able to resist teasing the director at the first run-through. The director asked, 'Mr Wayne, can you see your lines on the cue cards?'

'Gee,' Duke innocently replied, 'is that the size of the things? I don't think I can even see the cards!' This sent the director into a frenzy of anxiety before Duke laughingly calmed him down.

Cards or not, this is what Duke said that night:

Good evening. My name is John Wayne. I've come here tonight to pay my respects to our thirty-ninth president, our new commander in chief, and wish you Godspeed, sir, in the uncharted waters ahead.

Starting tomorrow at high noon, all of our hopes and our dreams go into that great house with you.

You've become our transition into the unknown tomorrow, and we're with you. Every one of us is with you.

I'm privileged to be present and accounted for in this capital of freedom, to watch a common man take on the uncommon responsibilities that he has won fair and square by stating his case to the American people, not by bloodshed or beheading or riots at the palace gates.

I'm considered a member of the opposition, the loyal opposition. Accent on the 'loyal.' I'd have it no other way.

In conclusion, may I add my voice to the millions of others round the world that wish you goodwill, Mr President.

We ask only one thing: that you preserve this one nation under God, with liberty and justice for all; and we know that you will, sir.

Thank you.

Duke hadn't written the original speech, but he'd gone over every line and revised it himself to fit his style. He meant every word he spoke, and the audience response was one of the warmest of the evening.

After the three-hour-long show we were ushered into a room where a receiving line had been organized. What I remember most vividly about that is what happened when Duke was spotted. Looking up, President-elect Carter saw Duke from across the room, and, breaking all protocol, he and Vice President-elect Mondale excused themselves, stepped out of the receiving line, and came over to shake his hand and thank him for coming.

My 'Southern buddy,' though, never did ask us for lunch.

We stayed east for a couple more weeks to attend several more luncheons and dinners and to sneak in a side trip to St Croix and visit Maureen O'Hara and her husband, Charlie Blair. Then it was back to California, and the end of our brief alliance with Jimmy Carter. Or so we thought.

Who could have guessed that just nine months later, the president and the Duke would be back again on the same side, and this time on an issue that was splitting conservatives and liberals all over the country.

Over the years Duke had built up a great many friendships with people in Panama. It had begun when he had married his first wife, Josephine, whose father had been consul general for Panama in the United States. Since then, Duke had visited there often, conducted many financial dealings with Panamanians, and struck up a great friendship with Arnulfo Arias, the former president of Panama. Arias' sons, Tony and Tito, themselves had had a business deal with Duke, and Tony Arias was even godfather to Aissa.

It was with dismay, then, that Duke observed the firestorm of criticism that exploded that fall when President Carter signed the treaties turning the Panama Canal officially over to Panama. He felt that Carter

113

had certainly been 'high-handed' in signing the treaties without giving Congress a chance to study them first, but he also felt there was no excuse for the 'hysteria' the conservatives were displaying.

In Duke's view, our own position in Panama was perfectly well protected by the treaties, and the 'sovereignty' claimed by opponents to the move was never something we had in the first place. As he wrote to one senator, 'We are giving a hospitable and friendly country what has never been ours—its honor, its dignity, and its pride; and we are keeping what is fundamental and vital to our national interest.'

Duke's position brought him into conflict with most other conservatives, and we got our own sampling of the 'hysteria' in the mail: hundreds of letters calling him everything from 'senile' to 'traitor.' In particular, it brought him up against his old friend Ronald Reagan, who was leading the opposition with the slogan, 'We built it, we paid for it, we own it.'

Duke desperately wanted to be in agreement with Reagan on this matter. He even wrote him a lengthy letter, mentioning all the things he had done for him over the years and saying, in effect, that the least Reagan could do was speak to their mutual friend Arturo McGowan, of Panama, and hear the real story.

I wasn't privy to Reagan's reply, but I do remember that Nancy Reagan phoned soon afterward, quite upset and hurt about Duke's letter. Duke called Reagan a day or so later, and although he did persuade him to see McGowan, it did absolutely no good. 'Even if he wanted to change his mind,' Duke said to me, 'he has gone so far in the other direction that it's too late.' Things were never again the same between those two old friends.

Nevertheless, Duke simply would not give up on Panama. Throughout that fall and winter I was at my typewriter transcribing long letters from Duke to senators, congressmen, generals, and newspaper editors. He was like a man obsessed. He kept dictating some days until he was too hoarse even to speak, too tired even to eat dinner.

In the end I don't know what effect Duke's letters may have had, but I do know that the publicity generated by his support was a big psychological boost for the president's side, and that Carter himself thanked Duke for what he had done.

On April 18, 1978, the Senate finally ratified the treaties, 68 to 32. Unfortunately, by then, Duke had much more serious matters on his mind.

CHAPTER 12

THROUGHOUT 1977 Duke's health was deteriorating badly. Each passing month brought new problems. He hated to give in to it, but he felt just lousy, and his medicine chest looked like a branch of the Newport pharmacy. At one point I began making charts and taping them on the mirror so he could check off what he had taken and when. There were so many medicines to remember: digitalis, digoxin, allopurinal, potassium; also, Lasix, for water retention, which, it turned out, had been the real source of much of his weight problem.

I remember we had been back from the inaugural for only a few days when Duke got word that Andy Devine, who had been battling leukemia, had died of cardiac arrest at the age of seventy. A longtime friend, Devine had known Duke long before *Stagecoach*, and they had appeared together in a number of films. They hadn't seen much of each other recently, but the gravel-voiced comedian had always been one of Duke's favorite people. Devine had requested cremation, his ashes to be strewn about up north, and a memorial service was planned for February 22 at Pacific View Memorial Park, in Newport. Duke and I were there to pay our last respects.

As we walked up the hill, with its breathtaking view of the bay, Duke said, 'When my time comes, this is where I plan to be.' It was a casual remark; there was nothing premonitory in his voice. Yet he had never discussed his death before—at least not with me—and those words chilled and frightened me. I forced myself to put them out of my mind, but it's not easy when

116

you see the man you love constantly gasping for breath and hear his voice diminish with hoarseness with each passing day.

And I wasn't doing much to help the situation. That May, just one day after Duke's seventieth birthday, I was soaping myself in the shower when I detected a lump in my breast.

Because of the great attention given to mastectomy over the previous few years, in addition to the hundreds of letters I had answered from cancer victims imploring Duke for help and advice, I automatically thought the worst.

Before leaving for work, I phoned my gynecologist and made an appointment for that afternoon, but I didn't want to alarm Duke needlessly. After we kissed good morning and went over the day's schedule, I cheerfully remarked that I'd have to tear myself away from my desk for an hour or two to keep an appointment with my gynecologist—some silly 'female problem.' I was deliberately vague, and Duke didn't question it. I kept cool, though, until my examination, when my gynecologist immediately phoned a thoracic surgeon and made an appointment for me the following day. He wanted a second opinion. Then it was panic time. On the way back to the house, I couldn't decide whether or not to tell Duke, but the minute he saw my face, he knew there was something terribly wrong.

'Out with it,' he demanded. When I finished my story, he said quietly, 'It could be nothing. But I'm going to that doc with you tomorrow and get some straight talk.'

Duke remained in the waiting room until the examination was over and I was dressed; then he joined us in the consulting room. There was no question about it. I had to have a biopsy, the sooner the better. Until the tissue was examined, no definite diagnosis could be made.

I guess I wasn't thinking straight, because I started crying. 'But my birthday is coming up next week and

117

we're going on a cruise to Catalina.' The fact that the biopsy would take only a short time and I'd not be hospitalized didn't matter. If something awful was found, they'd want to do immediate surgery.

Duke took over from there. He knew all the right questions. The doctor finally agreed that a week or so wouldn't make that much difference medically, but he thought I'd be better off mentally if I got it over with as quickly as possible. No, I didn't want to know—until after my birthday. Once Duke had been convinced that the delay would not result in any physical danger, he decided to go along with my wishes. But he added, 'You know, Pat, I have to leave for Mexicali as soon as we return from Catalina. That meeting was arranged months ago. I won't be able to be with you!' I knew. But I had a choice, and I chose to have a 'happy' birthday.

Duke made every effort to be comforting, reassuring, and cheerful during the cruise, but nothing helped. I got to the point where I couldn't even sit down for dinner without bursting into tears. I'd leave the table, and Duke would come after me, take me in his arms, dry my tears, and escort me back to the table. But I couldn't eat and I couldn't sleep. I'd stay awake, thinking, no more strapless gowns, no more bathing suits, no more bosoms, maybe no more Pat Stacy.

Duke had the patience of a saint, but finally my negative attitude got to him.

'If I knew you'd act this way,' he told me, 'I would have insisted you have that biopsy on the spot. Any number of things could have caused that lump, and it can disappear as suddenly as it appeared. So stop thinking you have the Big C.' But I couldn't stop thinking about it.

Shortly after we returned to Newport, Duke reluctantly flew down to Mexicali, and I entered the outpatient division of Hoag Hosptial for my biopsy. The gods were with me: it turned out negative. Duke called three times from Mexicali, and when he got back, he headed to my little house to make sure I was okay. A few days later a package arrived from Neiman-Marcus: a strapless black bathing suit, which Duke had ordered from their catalogue, with a card that said simply, 'I told you so!'

It wasn't until much later that he told me he had been a lot more worried than he had let on, but he hadn't wanted to add to my panic and so had kept cool.

It wasn't the sort of thing to ease Duke's mind, though, particularly after it became clear that he was suffering from a serious heart problem. Willing to try just about anything, he had gone to an acupuncturist, who had suspected his problems were cardiac-related and advised he see a cardiologist, which Duke had done immediately. I can't recall how many different tests were conducted, but the problem was finally traced to a defective mitral valve. As it was explained to me, the mitral valve is like a small parachute in the heart—and the strings had broken. No one knew exactly how or when it had happened, but there was a strong suspicion that it was due to all that heavy coughing Duke had done when he'd contracted walking pneumonia on that trip to England four years before. He may have been carrying it around with him all that time.

When I laid my head on his chest, I could hear a gushing sound around his heart.

Had Duke been younger, I'm certain he'd have been operated on immediately, but it was now considered a last-resort measure. No one wanted to put a seventy-year-old man with one lung under the knife, if there was any way to prevent it. Duke himself resisted the idea, optimistic that the drugs he was taking would turn the trick and enable him to function normally in spite of that damaged mitral valve. No matter how bad he felt, he just kept going.

By February, 1978, Duke's voice was so bad it was almost unrecognizable, and not even an appointment with a physician specializing in voices did any good. As we drove back from Beverly Hills that day, Duke refused to discuss the visit with me. He was in a horrible mood; it was raining so hard that we could barely see, and the windows were fogged up. I was terrified, and Duke drove the way he always drove. It was a minor miracle that we made it home safely.

For the rest of the month our life was governed by doctors' appointments of all kinds, but especially with the cardiologist. Duke still kept up with the business meetings at the house, but on several occasions, when he had guests over, he was forced to excuse himself and go to bed early—a really bad sign.

Still, Duke refused to give in. He kept making career commitments, planning for the future. He signed a two-year three-million-dollar exclusive contract with ABC to appear as himself in six two-hour spectaculars and in a couple of network's variety shows. 'The critics have accused me of doing nothing but playing John Wayne for years anyway,' he said, and laughed. 'Now it will be official!'

In addition, he'd come across a novel called *Beau John,* by Buddy Atkinson, which, though still in manuscript, excited him so much that he had Batjac buy it before it was even in galley proof. *Beau John* told the story of smalltown Kentucky life in the 1920s. Duke liked it for its native humor, and because it had a wonderful role for Ron Howard. Duke hadn't received that Oscar nomination for *The Shootist,* and he was hoping that *Beau John* would do the trick. Mentally, at least, he started making plans for its production.

Physically, however, he had to keep *Beau John* on the back burner. At the moment, he was very weak, so much so that he later admitted to a friend, 'I couldn't even pick up my makeup case.' In March we attended Skip Hathaway's surprise birthday party for her husband, Henry, who had directed *True Grit,* and Duke even made an effort to dance with Skip, but he had to leave the floor after a couple of minutes. Later he told me, 'I could hardly breathe.'

The only other engagement we kept that month, because Duke insisted on it, was the American Film Institute's Life Achievement Award banquet for Henry Fonda. Duke and Henry had been friends for so long that he was determined to make it, no matter how miserable he felt. He even had some special matchbooks made up and presented to Henry, the cover embossed with:

WANGER gave you *Stagecoach*
ZANUCK gave you *The Grapes of Wrath*
GOLDWYN gave you *Hurricane*
Now Merian C. Cooper brings you *Fort Apache*

Fort Apache had been the only movie in which Duke and Fonda had co-starred, back in 1948, and the two had had a running gag about it ever since.

That night, Duke and I were seated alongside each other throughout the ceremonies, and I've always felt that Shirlee Fonda, Henry's wife, had had a hand in ensuring that. Being the girl friend—or boy friend—of a star is never easy in Hollywood. You get your share of snickers and stares, and you're rarely considered more than an appendage of the man or woman you're accompanying. With the snickers come the snubs. I remember a banquet at which, instead of being seated with Duke as we had been told I'd be—I was stuck out in no-man's-land at a table of total strangers. There was nothing that could be done about it, but when we got back to our hotel, I exploded in frustration at Duke, tearing off my dress and throwing it down the stairs at him, saying, 'I don't know why you even bother taking me to these things if they treat me like some tenth-class citizen!'

Duke managed to calm me down that night, though he had been upset, too. But just a few months prior to the banquet for Henry Fonda, it had happened again, at a dinner for Elizabeth Taylor. At that dinner, however, Shirlee Fonda had come over to where I was sitting and whispered, 'I went through the same thing when Hank and I were going out.' She had been an airline stewardess when they'd met, and much younger than Henry. 'Don't worry about it,' she continued. 'If they want the man, then they must accept the woman. Meanwhile, Pat, there's room at our table. Won't you join us?' The 'us' included Paul Newman and Joanne Woodward, among others, and it turned out to be a lovely evening. Shirlee is a super lady. Duke and I understood why Henry always said one of the great sadnesses in his life was that he hadn't met Shirlee years before.

Although he was not feeling at all well, Duke seemed to enjoy the AFI party, and got a particular kick over the fact that Jane Fonda's children came over to the table to ask for his autograph. Politically, of course, there had been a great friction between Duke and Jane, but personally he liked her a lot, even if he felt, as he said, that her thinking was 'all mixed up.'

On St Patrick's Day, Duke met with several of his doctors, all of whom emphasized the necessity of his checking into Hoag Hospital the following Monday. Duke's weight was still going up, and the water-retention problem was alarming. By now, surgery—the last alternative—was mandatory.

Four days later Dr Joel Manchester performed an angiogram, a heart X ray done with the aid of an iodine solution injected into the body, which projects a perfect picture of the cardiac area. The angiogram in itself was risky—many patients have gone into cardiac arrest during the process—but it had to be done to ascertain whether or not Duke could be considered a candidate for surgery. The mitral valve *had* to be replaced; because of his age and condition, the question was whether or not he could survive the trauma.

Duke was still hospitalized at Hoag on Easter Sunday, a dreary day for us all, but by now it had been decided that the operation should be performed by a specialist

My first birthday with Duke, June 6, 1973, aboard the *Wild Goose*, while Duke was making *McQ*. It was on the set of *McQ* that the electricity first began. Two crew men look on. (Bert Minshall)

Duke's seventy-first birthday, May 26, 1978. He was already back at work-that very same day, he appeared live via satellite on a Bob Hope special. (Kathy Mihalovich)

Aboard the *Wild Goose,* summer 1976, with Victoria, British Columbia, in the background. After three months of gruelling work and bouts with ill health, it was time for some well-deserved rest and relaxation.

Manzanillo, Mexico, winter 1977, aboard the *Wild Goose*. By this time we knew Duke needed heart surgery. (Bert Minshall)

Duke and Lauren Bacall on the set of *The Shootist*, February 1976. Duke played an ageing gunfighter dying of cancer — a sadly prophetic role.

Duke, as the world knew him. (Pat Stacy)

Running the gauntlet of photographers at the 1977 Scopus Award for humanitarianism. Duke was being honoured. (Hans Reigl)

On a visit to Panama, January 1978. Despite the impending surgery, Duke insisted on working hard for the Panama Canal treaties — to the dismay of conservatives. (Joe DeFranco)

August 1978, taken during a break in filming a Great Western Savings & Loan commercial.

Me, friend Chick Iverson, Marisa, Duke, and Ethan by the pool at Duke's home. Duke's moustache was for his role in *The Shootist*.

Easter 1979. Duke's last cruise on the *Wild Goose* to Catalina Island.
(Bert Minshall)

at Boston's Massachusetts General Hospital, considered to be the best-equipped hospital in the country for this kind of surgery.

I was given a book, *Surgeon Under the Knife,* by Dr William A. Nolen, to prepare for what lay ahead. I wanted to know everything, to brace myself for the ordeal.

For three days prior to our leaving for Boston, Duke was permitted to spend the afternoon at his house, on the condition that he eat nothing other than hospital-supervised meals and return to Hoag for the night. It was an unusual arrangement, but it gave us a chance to make plans for the months ahead. There was so much to do; it was almost like a secret military mission.

Michael and Patrick agreed to act as an advance guard, and headed for Boston early to take care of all the necessary arrangements at the hospital, as well as to find accommodations for the rest of the family and me. There was never any question about my coming along. Aissa, Toni, Melinda, and Duke's friends Joe DeFranco and Jack Gordean also planned to be in Boston during this crucial time, but Duke decided the younger children should remain in Newport with their mother. He didn't want to interrupt their schooling, and he felt the strain might be too much for them.

We had been considering chartering a private plane east when Ross McClintock, a top official of the Fluor Corporation, a plant-construction firm with headquarters in Irvine, suggested that since he was flying east on business, we should join him on the company's private G-2. The plane was outfitted in such a way that Duke could nap comfortably through most of the trip.

Early on March 29, Barney drove us to the Orange County Airport. I later found out that the pilots had been given a sealed envelope and had no idea of the identities of the other passengers or our destination until we boarded the plane.

We knew we could't keep the news of Duke's impending surgery concealed from the press indefinitely, but he was desperate to avoid reporters and photographers at this point in his life. He simply wasn't up to answering questions or being photographed. The trip itself was strain enough.

As we circled Logan Airport, coming into Boston, I refused to accept the unacceptable. But, looking back, I wonder if we all weren't thinking the same thought: how long would it be until we'd be making that trip back home again, and whether Duke would be making it with us.

Part III
Crashing

CHAPTER 13

DUKE was characteristically uncommunicative during the twenty-minute drive from Logan Airport to Massachusetts General. Patrick and Michael had briefed us thoroughly, and none of us was in the mood for small talk. Because of the boys' presence, I stifled my longing to put my arms around Duke and hold him so tightly that by some magical osmosis my youth and energy would be transferred to him. Every so often during that interminable trip, however, I placed my hand on his and he responded with a gentle squeeze and a loving glance.

As we drove through the back gate of Massachusetts General, the grounds were completely deserted, no press or photographers anywhere. We knew we couldn't keep Duke's admittance to the hospital a secret forever, but we were playing for time and praying for privacy.

A hospital aide escorted Duke to his room in Phillips House 8, the best accommodations available. Millionaires, movie stars, and later even Henry Kissinger would stay here, but it was obvious Massachusetts General kept its focus on medical care and not on luxury.

The room had no air conditioning and no screens on the windows, the furniture consisted of an iron bed, a nightstand, a chair, and a small closet. It was dismal and depressing, but Duke just shrugged, 'What the hell, I'm not going to remain here forever.' For a while, however, it seemed as if he were.

I was still with Duke when Dr Roman DeSanctis, who would be Duke's cardiologist there, arrived to begin what would be the start of an interminable number of presurgical tests. One of them involved Duke's blowing into an odd little machine to determine how much lung power he had. When that test was completed, Duke told Dr DeSanctis, quite firmly, 'I want Miss Stacy to know everything that's going on. I want her to be treated as a family member. She's to be allowed to visit at all times, and whatever you tell my children, tell her.'

There were tests and more tests and still more tests, but no one told us the results, and our anxieties mounted. The surgical plan had been to replace Duke's faulty mitral valve with a valve from a pig's heart, which was generally considered the safest and most effective substitute. Two days after his admittance, however, Duke learned that the doctors were still uncertain whether the benefit from the valve replacement would justify the risk involved. The operation had a two- to twenty-five-percent risk factor, and owing to Duke's age and the chronic bronchitis, the prognosis for him was a ten-percent risk. The doctors were hesitant about taking even that much of a chance, and continued to delay scheduling surgery.

Michael, Patrick, Duke, and I kept asking questions, but we couldn't get straight answers. The evasiveness and delays played havoc with our nerves. Duke's mood alternated between irritability and depression, and when he was in that frame of mind, he wanted to be alone.

When I bade him goodnight on the evening of March 30, he said, 'Dammit, Pat, tomorrow is Aissa's birthday. Some celebration she's going to have, sitting around in this place.' I told him Jack Gordean had planned a luncheon party for Aissa and that we'd all be there trying to make the day as cheerful as possible. 'Make sure to hand her a couple of hundred to buy something pretty,' he said.

We all did our best for Aissa on her birthday, but we were all conscious of the 'empty chair' at the table, and Aissa seemed the most stricken, all nerves and terribly lonely.

When we returned from visiting Duke that evening, she asked, 'Pat, would you mind terribly if I shared your room with you? It's simply awful being alone. I know I'll sleep better if someone is in the same room with me.'

'We'll *both* sleep better,' I replied.

Aissa kept her room across the hall but used it only to shower and dress. For the rest of her stay in Boston we were roommates, and that helped us both to get through the ordeal.

When I arrived at the hospital the next morning, I presented Duke with a cute little card I had found. It had a piglet on the cover, and on the inside it read, 'I thought of you at dinner last night.'

He gave a perfunctory glance and said, 'Well, you'll be thinking about me more when we have dinner together tonight.'

I was perplexed. It was against all hospital regulations for visitors to dine with patients—in fact, I felt grateful when a nurse brought me a cup of coffee—and they'd never allow Duke to go out to dinner. Or—and I paused—did it mean that the medical team had decided the operation was too risky after all? Was Duke being discharged? Had the entire, agonizing trip been for nothing?

Suddenly Duke grinned, and it hit me. It was April 1.

'April Fool, yourself,' I said angrily.

'April Fool, my ass,' Duke replied. 'We're all going out to dinner tonight—you, me, the kids, the whole gang who've been hanging around in the hallway since I've been here. The pig is being led to slaughter. All systems are go for Monday morning, but meanwhile let's live it up a little'.

I found out later how the decision had been reached. The previous day, Duke's patience had finally reached its breaking point. He wanted that operation, he had

128

told Dr DeSanctis; he wanted that chance, and if it killed him, that was the chance he was taking. Making his point dramatically, he had ordered, 'Open that window. You're going to operate on me or so help me I'm going to jump out. Measure your risk factors for that!' No one had dared to call Duke's bluff. The doctors had decided to operate.

As for Duke's being permitted to dine out, the doctors felt the benefit to Duke's battered morale would more than compensate for any upset diet or minor drain on his energy. One of the doctors had even taken it upon himself to arrange for a private room at Maison Robert, a restaurant located in what had been Boston's old City Hall.

Duke and I arrived by private limousine. His children and friends were already there. We had agreed to make the evening as cheerful and undemanding on Duke as possible.

They all had had a predinner cocktail already, to avoid drinking in Duke's presence, but he demanded a martini, and was furious when we protested that he shouldn't drink. With equal vehemence he countered, 'One drink is not going to kill me,' and before the discussion could become a heated argument, Patrick left the table to call Duke's doctor.

Patrick returned from the phone, grinning.

'It's okay, Dad. You can have your drink—but just one for the entire evening.'

Duke ordered—'the largest martini your bartender can concoct'— and when the drink came, he insisted on making the toast. Looking around at the almost ecclesiastical atmosphere of the room, with its stained-glass windows and heavy wood tables, he rose, raised his glass, and proclaimed, 'To the last supper.'

Almost in unison we murmured, 'Oh, Duke.'

In truth he had voiced what we were all thinking, all fearing, but none of us wanted to drink to *that*. I believe it was Joe DeFranco who emended the toast: 'Last supper till Newport.' That broke the tension, and for a

129

few hours, at least, we all tried to pretend that we *were* indeed in Newport without a care in the world.

Duke had griped about having to return to his hospital bed by midnight, but as usual he had overestimated his stamina. We took leave of the party at ten-thirty and were back at Massachusetts General by eleven P.M.

The nurse at the night desk informed me that, as usual, the switchboard had been buzzing all evening with calls from press and fans trying to get through to Duke's room, and that one particularly persistent guy had called a half-dozen times claiming he was Frank Sinatra. Since we found it had become a frequent ruse to call using somebody else's name, just in the hope of getting through, we didn't rush to the phone. As it turned out, though, it had been Frank, who had read an erroneous report that Duke was undergoing immediate surgery and had been calling all night to find out about his condition.

On Sunday afternoon Duke's family and I met with Dr DeSanctis and Dr Mortimer Buckley for a detailed description of the mitral-valve-replacement process. We were given a plastic valve to examine and were told exactly where and how the surgery would be performed.

Dr DeSanctis made a special effort to assure us that the heart was merely another organ of the body, no different from a liver, lung, or kidney. Poetry and romantic propaganda to the contrary, he said, one didn't love with the heart or feel with the heart; nothing emotional was being violated because of heart surgery. I was very impressed by that. Somehow it meant a great deal to me. I wanted to ask Dr DeSanctis, 'What do we love with, then? Our minds? Our souls?' But there was a far more important question to be answered: how much danger was really involved? The risk factor hadn't changed, but both doctors assured us we had every reason to be optimistic.

We were permitted a few moments with Duke before they began preparing him for the next day's surgery;

then we were requested to return to the hotel, and Dr De Sanctis tactfully suggested it would be best if only Michael and I were at the hospital prior to the morning operation. If everything went as well as expected, the rest of the family could join us once the operation was actually in progress. No other visitors would be permitted.

Michael, Patrick, and I were at the hospital by daybreak. Surprisingly, we were allowed to see Duke before he was wheeled into the operating room. I kissed him, and told him I'd see him later. In his semidrugged state he whispered back, 'Ten horsemen left, but only nine came back . . .'

It had been estimated the Duke would be in surgery for approximately three hours, and arrangements had been made for Michael and me and the rest of the family to remain in a private office. Every so often, someone on the staff came in to tell us that things were progressing well. Duke had been put on an automatic heart machine during the valve replacement. Sometimes the patient's own heart fails to start up again, but finally Dr DeSanctis popped his head through the door to tell us that Duke was back on his own heart, and it was working perfectly. Immensely cheered, we phoned Duke's friends back at the hotel to tell them the good news.

DeSanctis had warned us about what to expect when we saw Duke again, but it was still a traumatic sight. Duke was unconscious, strapped down to his bed so he wouldn't move when he came out of the anesthetic, with several different tubes down his throat and attached to his body.

But he was going to be all right. He had lived through the surgery.

After a little while we realized there was nothing more we could do at the hospital, so after informing Duke's friends of the operation's outcome, Aissa and I returned to my room and finally succumbed to the pressure we had been under. We passed out on the beds.

Michael, meanwhile, decided it was finally time for a

press conference, and the news was released. When I got back to the hospital, there were dozens of phone messages waiting, most of them from names that were unrecognizable: newspaper people, television and radio reporters, well-wishers.

I recall turning on the radio and hearing Duke's surgery reported as the top story of the hour. Besides the details of the operation, the report rehashed Duke's bout with cancer and ended with the note that Duke would be missed at the Oscar ceremonies that evening. As if that mattered!

I had totally forgotten about the Oscar telecast that night. Neither Aissa nor I was much in the mood for it, but I thought Duke might like to hear what happened when he was feeling better, so we turned it on.

The show went along at its usual pace, then, somewhere toward the end, Bob Hope unexpectedly faced the cameras and said, solemnly, 'We want you to know, Duke, we miss you tonight. We expect you to amble out here in person next year, because there is no one who can fill John Wayne's boots.'

It was so lovely I almost cried.

Although I had very much wanted to be with Duke the moment he regained consciousness, it didn't work out that way. Nurse Rhoda Bates was the first person he saw, and we learned later that he was totally disoriented. Because of the liquid flowing into him, he felt he was drowning; he was convinced he was dying.

Nurse Bates rubbed his forehead and told him repeatedly, 'Duke you're going to be all right, you're going to be all right.' And he fell back into a deep sleep.

I can't recall how many trips I made to Massachusetts General that day, though Duke was unaware of any of them. He was tucked away in a small cubicle at the rear of the intensive-care unit, to ensure his privacy, and the security was tight. The children and I were the only ones permitted to enter the ICU, and even then only two of us at a time. Duke was still not permitted visits from his friends. There are too many of them on top of the family, Dr DeSanctis protested. The men decided to pack and return home, and we all talked cheerfully about a grand reunion in Newport Beach.

Now that Duke was progressing satisfactorily, his doctor turned his attention to Aissa and me. We both looked awful, he said. If we didn't get away from the hospital and have some fun, he'd have two additional patients to contend with. 'Go shopping; go sightseeing; take in a show. There are a hundred things two pretty girls can do in Boston. You can't be of any help to Duke right now, and it will be much better for him if you're both in good shape when he's convalescing.' It was easier for him to say than for us to do, but we promised to fill the prescription. When Melinda and Toni left for Los Angeles on April 5, it was just Aissa and myself, alone.

Although there was a fifteen-year age gap between us, somehow it never felt like it. Were it not for the shadow of Duke's condition, we might have been sorority sisters off on a spring holiday. We'd sit in my room, have a drink or two, talk about clothes and dieting, and experiment with the oversupply of exotic makeup we'd just bought. One night we went wild and emerged looking like members of a punk-rock group. It was silly, and kid stuff, but it gave us something to do, something to laugh about, and it relieved the tension of just waiting around.

Aissa confided in me about her current boy friend, and we frequently phoned friends back home. I'm sure she kept her mother advised of Duke's progress—Pilar was as concerned about Duke's health as any of us—but those calls were made in the privacy of her own room. Aissa never discussed her mother with me, and she was far too tactful to ask any questions about my personal relationship with her father.

She knew, however, that Duke and I were more than companions, that we loved each other deeply, and I was terribly touched when she said to me one night, 'Oh,

Pat, you don't know how thankful I am for you, how grateful that you are here to be with my dad.'

Aissa also confided that when she had been a little girl, her dad had told her, 'If anything ever happens to me, just look up and find a big star in the sky. That will be me. I'll always be there watching over you.'

CHAPTER 14

As anxious as I was about Duke's condition, I was still his secretary, and in the days to come I had my work cut out for me.

The wires and flowers had started arriving right after the Oscar telecast—I'd brought the wires back to the hotel and sent the bouquets to the children's and geriatric wards—but now the deluge really began: hundreds of cards, letters, and miniature pigs. The pig's heart had not gone without notice. The mail arrived daily in huge U.S. Mail bags: what to do with it all? The mailroom at the hospital had no facilities for storage, we didn't want to forward it unopened to Newport Beach—Duke would have been furious—and it was impractical to drag it back to the Holiday Inn.

The most sensible solution was to send it up to Duke's old room in Phillips 8 and keep it there until he returned. The idea didn't sit well with the executive staff, since there was a long waiting list for beds at Massachusetts General; but after much persuasion, they agreed to the arrangement when I promised to open, read, and select with record speed the items Duke would want to see. For every bag of mail I got through, however, two more seemed to take its place!

On the morning of April 6 I headed for the hospital to see Duke, and by chance ran into Andy McLaglen, who had directed Duke in *McLintock* in 1963 and who was on the floor visiting another friend. Naturally he wanted to see Duke. I told him about the 'family only' rule, but I thought I might be able to sneak him into Duke's cubicle for a few minutes. I had no idea what shape I would find Duke in, but, to my delight, he was actually sitting up in bed, and the tube that had prevented his talking had been removed. The first words I heard from his mouth since they had wheeled him into surgery were, 'There's my girl in the pretty pink dress.' How typical of Duke to notice! I wanted to rush to his side to kiss him, but to reduce the risk of infection, it was still forbidden. Instead I just squeezed his ankle gently, and that served the same purpose.

Duke was able to sit up for an hour and a half that day. Aissa and Michael went in together, and we managed to sneak Andy in for a few minutes. (Later I found out that Duke remembered none of this. He thought he had *dreamed* McLaglen was there.) He was obviously still hazy that morning, but he seemed so much better, and Dr DeSanctis boosted our morale even further when he told us they were planning to remove Duke from the ICU in a day or two and transfer him to yet another building, Baker 12, which was something of a halfway house between the intensive-care unit and Phillips, where he would convalesce.

'Convalesce'—what a beautiful, optimistic word.

'By the way,' DeSanctis added with a straight face, 'our friend almost caused a riot here last night.' It seemed that the wife of another patient had taken a wrong turn and entered Duke's cubicle by mistake. When she'd reached the head of the bed, she had let out a piercing cry: 'That's not my husband! That's John Wayne!' She had been so unraveled, the nurses swore it took twenty minutes to calm her down.

After I left Duke's room that morning, I headed for his old room at Phillips, where I spent the rest of the day, well into dinnertime, trying to devise an efficient, workable system to handle the mail. At first I tried opening the letters and screening them, but that took so long that I just concentrated on what were obviously get-well cards. The pig theme was evident here, too. I made sure to put the return address of the sender on each card, since I knew Duke would insist on thank-you

136

notes. In addition, I had to be careful to sort out mail from Duke's friends and co-workers first, because I knew he'd want to hear about those right away. I worked on and on, but it was like bailing out the *Titanic* with an ice bucket! There had to be some system to establish order from this chaos. Finally I decided just to look at the names and return addresses. If I recognized them, I'd pull the letter; if not, it went into a box, to be opened when we got home and could hire a staff to help. It wasn't the best system in the world—an adorable card from Duke's grandson Christopher was overlooked because he didn't have his name on the envelope—but there was no other solution.

I read the wires and some of the letters to Duke, and tried to convey the enormity of the mail coming in, but he thought I was exaggerating and just trying to make him feel good. It wasn't until some press people got wind of the public response and asked if they could send some photographers over that I finally saw a way to convince him. The hospital staff had finally been able to clear out a small storeroom next to the mail room and told me I could use it as a temporary office as long as Duke was at Massachusetts General, so I held a small press conference in my 'office,' and the chaos was recorded for posterity—and for Duke's personal benefit.

We were all relieved when Duke was moved into Baker 12. After the ICU his room looked like the Ritz, and with all those horrible tubes removed, he looked like Duke again. They were still strict about his having to rest, but usually I would get there by seven A.M., so I would be with him when he awakened, stay a while, wander over to Phillips House to work on the mail, make a couple more trips back to Baker, and then join Aissa. The doctors had to tell Duke they had forbidden us to be there constantly; he wanted someone around all the time.

Meanwhile, he was making an excellent recovery. For one thing, his normal voice had returned! It was an unexpected side benefit, something to do with a nerve and his larynx. I didn't understand the details, but the upshot was that the surgery had taken care of his voice problem. Duke later told me he had almost been more worried about his voice than his heart, because the former was a tool of his trade. He sounded like John Wayne again now, not a hoarse imitation. He was warned not to tire himself out by talking too much, so we kept conversation to a minimum, but we did have a phone temporarily installed in his room so he could talk to Ethan and Marisa. At one point Duke had to assure Marisa repeatedly that although he was sleeping a great deal, he had never been in a coma. We couldn't understand why that was such a great worry, until we found out that Bert Minshall, the skipper of *Wild Goose*, had taken her to see the movie *Coma* during the period when Duke hadn't been able to phone her. When Duke heard about that, he blew his top.

Of course, in a way, his blowing his top was a good sign. When Duke began to gripe again, we knew he was feeling better. Another good sign was that he was on his feet again and walking a little longer and farther each day. It wasn't training for the Boston Marathon, perhaps, but at this stage of his recovery the ability to make it to the bathroom by himself was an achievement.

On April 14 Duke had some root-canal work performed by the hospital's resident dentist. (Imagine going through root-canal work after just having had heart surgery!) One of his teeth was badly infected, and there was nothing he could do about it. Then, over the weekend of April 16, he was wheeled out of Baker and back into Phillips. It was time for the real convalescence to begin.

Aissa had made plans to go home as soon as Duke was into Phillips, and now she prepared to leave. As we bade each other good-bye, I said, 'Don't worry about Duke.'

She replied, 'Pat, I don't have to worry about my dad. You are here with him.'

After she left, my days were busy as usual, but the

nights were bleak and lonely. Duke asked, 'Are Michael and Patrick including you in on everything?' But I brushed aside his question, saying, 'Look they're two fellows, and they really don't want me tagging along.' We did have a lovely time a few days later, though, when Duke managed to persuade the administration staff to bend their rules and let him have a dinner party for Michael and Gretchen, Patrick, and me in his room. It was a steak-and-lobster feast catered by Anthony's Pier 4 Restaurant, and one of the happiest times we had at Massachusetts General.

Duke's improvement was so astonishing by this time that all his doctors began paying social calls with their families. Dr DeSanctis' daughter had been to Monument Valley and photographed it, and one day she came in with a transparency three feet wide, which she had put together herself, and taped it to Duke's window. When the sun was shining, he had a gorgeous view of one of his favorite places in the world.

I detected my own signs of improvement as well. When Duke demanded I bring him a supply of catalogues and he began circling the items he wanted, I knew he was his old self again. One of the things he couldn't get from the catalogues, though, was a set of rubber rafts for the *Goose*, the kind he was certain were used by Gloucester fishermen. Consequently, I had to go to the other end of town, pay for them, and lug them back to the hospital mailroom to ship home along with the rest of his mail. The upshot of that, of course, was that the rafts were stolen in Newport before Barney could haul them to the *Goose*; what's more, after we got back I found the exact duplicates being sold in every discount shop in the San Pedro— Newport Beach area. So much for Gloucester fishermen!

By now we were counting the days until Duke was released from the hospital. In spite of his remarkable progress, there were still major problems to overcome.

The pain from the incision hadn't disappeared; nor had his coughing spells.

Someone on the staff had made a little pillow with the words 'Hug Me' on it for Duke to hold to his chest, and that was a great help when he started coughing. A little pounding on the back also helped get the mucus up. It was a technique I'd learned long ago from a therapist, who'd shown me how to start low and work my way upward to relieve the congestion. I had to be more careful now, though: Duke could feel the movement, and was apprehensive that the incision on his chest would break. I had to keep reassuring him that the doctors wouldn't have allowed it if they thought it would prove dangerous.

You worry about one thing; then something totally bizarre happens. On April 22, while casually eating a banana, Duke knocked a cap off a tooth and swallowed it. Chaos ensued. He demanded the nurses find it for him using—to put it politely—the same methods employed by custom inspectors to uncover swallowed contraband. Thank God he didn't ask me to make sure they were following his instructions. I would have done almost anything for Duke—but there are limits. Whether the nurses did as ordered or not, the cap was never found.

All annoyance vanished, however, when Dr DeSanctis at last brought us the news we had been praying for: on April 27, just two days short of a month after our arrival at Massachusetts General, Duke would be officially discharged. Such excitement! There was so much to do and so little time in which to get it all done; Duke wanted me with him constantly, but there was all the mail to box, label, and ship to California. Duke was still determined to answer every card and letter.

Patrick and Michael handled the travel logistics and the press. We all wanted to keep our departure as quiet as our arrival. The Fluor plane was due back in the Boston area and once again was generously put at our disposal.

Finally, everything was in order—almost. Without warning, Duke became apprehensive about leaving the Boston area. 'What if an unexpected complication sets in? Wouldn't it be wiser if we stuck around town a little longer?' he asked. He started to pore over the real-estate ads to see if he could find a sublet, and if Dr DeSanctis had not finally convinced him that he'd recuperate much faster in familiar surroundings, we might have stayed in Boston for weeks more. Then, when Dr DeSanctis agreed to join us on the plane ride home, everything was settled.

Almost. Sometime during that night, Duke had another brainstorm. When I entered his room at seven A.M., he was wide awake and champing at the bit. 'Get me a limo,' he said. 'I want to get out of here and drive out to Lexington and Concord.' Suddenly he wanted to go sightseeing. I called Dr DeSanctis, who saw no harm in his taking the excursion, but he suggested as a precaution that we take Duke's private nurse with us as well. The quiet ride into the country became a family outing when Michael, Patrick, and Gretchen decided to join us, too.

Duke, of course, insisted on leaving the car to explore all the picturesque shops in the area. The storekeepers went into near shock at the sight of him. Many of them no doubt had heard about the operation, but no one expected to see him meandering around in this neck of the woods. I can't recall everything we bought, but it seemed we cornered the market in T-shirts, which he wanted for himself and friends and family back home. When we were alone for a few minutes I remember asking, 'Duke, did you *really* want to see where the first shot of the Revolutionary War rang out, or were you using this as an excuse for another shopping expedition?'

He seemed hurt that I would be suspicious of his motives. 'Now, Pat, you know I've never been in this part of the country before, and who knows when I'll

141

get back here again.' I wasn't convinced, but it was wonderful seeing him have such a good time.

Actually, though I teased Duke, I understood why he had wanted to make this little excursion. From the time we arrived in Boston, with the exception of those few hours at Maison Robert, his life had been one hospital room after another. There would be no way that Duke, or any of us, could erase the memory of what he had gone through in the past month, but when he got home, he wanted to be able to discuss cheerful things with Ethan and Marisa, to shower them with amusing gifts and assure them that in spite of his operation he had been having an exciting adventure. Those souvenirs from Lexington and Concord would be happy reminders.

Hospital souvenirs he didn't need, but he came home with those, too. Before we left, the doctors and nurses who had tended Duke with such dedication held a farewell party in his honor and presented him with a mitral valve encased in Lucite and a little pewter dish with MASSACHUSETTS GENERAL HOSPITAL printed on it. Duke was overcome with emotion. He just sat there, and tears welled up in his eyes as he thanked the staff for the gifts, and for their care, and above all for their patience.

'I can't begin to tell you how grateful I am to all of you,' he said, adding, 'I think you'll all understand if I don't suggest we do it all over again sometime.'

We sneaked out of Massachusetts General by a downstairs delivery entrance early the next morning. Our departure date had been kept secret, but some newspapers must have had their photographers on around-the-clock shifts, for as we drove up the ramp, the flashbulbs started popping. Duke waved to the lensmen but wouldn't stop the car, and we were practically chased to Logan Airport, escaping only when the airport guards closed the gates to the private terminal.

142

Bob Fluor, who was returning West with us, had thought of everything to make the flight as comfortable as possible for Duke: even the sofa had been made up so Duke would be able to recline, which he did for most of the flight. In San Francisco, Fluor deplaned, and we saw a jostling horde of photographers lined up behind the fence. Evidently the word had spread that Duke was en route home, though how they knew the plane would be stopping in San Francisco was something we never learned.

We expected the same sort of thing at Orange County Airport, but, to our delight, there was no shouting or pushing; the photographers and reporters there behaved as if they were a welcoming committee rather than newsmen out for an exclusive.

Duke's California doctor, Robert Egan, was at the airport, as were Melinda and Aissa. Duke kept waving to everyone, then hugging the girls. More waving. More hugging.

And finally we were safely back on Bayshore Drive. Duke went straight to his room, eager to be back in his bed, in his house. It was still light, and as he sat up with his head propped against the pillows, he looked younger and happier than he had in years.

Even though Dr Egan had arranged for around-the-clock nurses, I remained at Duke's that evening, and throughout the night, to answer phone calls or just to be within shouting distance in case he needed me. During the month that had passed, I had been afraid to think of the future. As I settled in for the night in the guest room, however, my thoughts were on the beautiful summer ahead, a summer to be spent resting and relaxing in the sun. I intended to force Duke to take it easy, and when autumn came, we'd turn our attention to *Beau John*.

No more hospitals, no more suffering or fears. I even wondered, now that he had been given another chance at life, if he might not consider taking another chance at married life. He may have told the press he

143

wouldn't marry again, but he had never said that to me, not in so many words.

I faced the realization that I wanted to be Duke's wife, but only if that was what he wanted. If not, I was satisfied to remain with him as a loving companion and secretary, knowing that I had more time with him than most wives would, that I shared his work, his problems, his playtime.

I was ready to face whatever the future might bring. Except what the future eventually did bring.

CHAPTER 15

DUKE was home, and Newport's nautical contingent gave its returning hero a welcome reminiscent of Mac-Arthur and the Philippines.

Sunday, April 30, was the day of Newport's annual boat parade, and the entire flotilla sailed slowly past our private pier, flags waving, whistles blowing, with a huge banner proclaiming WELCOME HOME, DUKE. The kids and Joe and Barbara DeFranco joined Duke and me on the patio to watch the glorious show. It was an afternoon none of us would ever forget. Duke sat waving to the cheering crowd, his eyes moist, but he had a huge grin on his face.

In a scene from Duke's 1945 war epic, *They Were Expendable*, he eloquently read from Robert Louis Stevenson's poem, 'Requiem,' whose words mark the poet's tombstone: 'Home is the sailor, home from the sea,/And the hunter home from the hill.' It was one of Duke's favourite poems, and those words, too, came floating by, painted on a huge sign facing our pier. I doubt the boat's captain knew what the words really meant, but no matter. Duke was home neither from the sea nor from the hill but from the brink of that great unknown. And he had found a safe harbor—we were all so sure of that. He had been examined and reexamined, tested and retested, cut open and sewn together. How could anything else be wrong? Post-operative rest was all he needed to be his old self again.

Meanwhile, that damn pile of mail was still staring me in the face. We added two temporary secretaries to help Julie, Kathy, and me, but it was still impossible to make a dent in it. Finally Duke decided that maybe we should just make a list of the names and addresses of everyone who'd written, and he'd see to it that they got invitations or passes to his next film. He was still determined that that film would be *Beau John,* but suddenly he was having problems getting the project in motion. He never told me why—but I'm sure apprehension about Duke's health was a big factor.

If he couldn't get a movie going, then, by God, he'd do something on television. The doctors had told him to take it easy, but it was an impossible promise for him to keep. Duke lived to work. When Bob Hope asked him to narrate a segment of his seventy-fifth-birthday special coming up at the end of May—a USO tribute—Duke leaped at the opportunity, particularly since he could do his segment live via satellite from Newport. He wouldn't even have to leave the house.

It was Duke's first public appearance since his heart surgery, and he looked absolutely marvelous. With the exception of some slight hoarseness in his voice, he sounded wonderful, too, as he extolled the virtues of the USO between film clips of Hope's decades of entertaining troops all over the world.

Then Hope came on and, noting that Duke was just celebrating his own birthday, added, 'Everyone here and across America wish you many, many, many more, Duke . . . and, well, Duke, I hope I look as good as you do when I'm *your* age'.

Duke replied, 'You did.'

'No, I mean it,' Hope said. 'It's so good to see you looking so great.'

'Well, Bob,' Duke replied again, 'I hope you live forever; I really mean this, too. I hope you live forever, and mine is the last voice you hear.'

The audience roared, but Hope got in the last salvo.

'I know he's in good shape, because when he left the hospital he offered to shoot it out for the bill. I'm glad that it worked, that valve of the pig. Of course,

146

the pig's out beating up Indians—but he's a beautiful man, I'll tell you that.'

And everyone had to agree: he was a beautiful man. Certainly we all agreed at home that night of his birthday—a gala affair with a dozen of his best friends all around him to wish Duke a happy and healthy seventy-first. But health was something that just didn't seem to be in the cards for Duke.

I suspected something was amiss when Duke didn't drink all his wine that night, but I attributed it to overexertion. Not about to waste good wine, Arturo McGowan, and Joe DeFranco, and I turned Duke's glass into a loving cup for luck. Duke remained listless for much of the week that followed, but we still weren't particularly worried. He had no alarming symptoms, and he had been on a blood thinner after our return from Boston. Since alcohol causes the blood to become even thinner, I thought perhaps he had celebrated his birthday a bit too much even before he had called a halt to the wine.

Nevertheless, we brought him into Hoag Hospital for a routine checkup. The next thing we knew, the phone rang, and we got the verdict: hepatitis! Not contagious, unless anyone had had direct contact with the sick person, such as kissing or drinking from the same glass.

Since I had been guilty of both transgressions, I was told to get a gamma-globulin shot immediately, and, remembering that birthday-party 'loving cup,' I called the McGowans and DeFrancos and urged them to do the same. Where had it come from? Nobody knew. One theory was that Duke could have picked it up from one of the blood transfusions at Massachusetts General, but that was just speculation. I know the hospital had been meticulous in checking the blood donors, and it made little difference anyway. The point was, he had the damn disease, and we had to concentrate on arresting it.

That meant six weeks of rest, new medication,

absolutely no drinking, and daily visits from his doctor.

I had been planning a trip back home to see my parents in late June, but Duke insisted I might as well take it now. 'Look,' he said, 'I have to stay in bed. You went through enough of that nursing routine in Boston. Why don't you go ahead and visit your parents? Kathy and Julie can handle the secretarial duties.' I was reluctant to leave, but the sooner I went, the quicker I'd return, so I took the 'red-eye' to Louisiana on June 4 and was back in Newport by the twelfth.

Duke was still confined to his bed, but itching to get out, and somehow, in my absence, he had convinced his doctors that he'd be able to get as much rest on the *Wild Goose* as at home, and so had been given permission to cruise to Catalina on June 15—with the stipulation that he return for an examination and blood tests by the twentieth. Done! We had a very happy, relaxed five days. Marisa, Ethan, and my niece Shannon, who was visiting from Louisiana, were aboard, after being fortified with gamma globulin, and the kids kept themselves busy swimming and exploring while Duke and I just lazed around on deck. No pressure, no arguments, no interruptions. Hepatitis or not, this was the perfect way to spend the summer.

As promised, we were back in the doctor's office on the twentieth, where the doctor noted a marked improvement in Duke's condition, and then it was back out again on the *Goose* for another week of lazy sailing, this time with several of Duke's friends.

We had no definite schedule except for meals. It was left to each person to decide when to arise, when to retire. At times I would read until three A.M., hoping to sleep late. Always an early riser, Duke was usually up and dressed by six-thirty or seven. He'd peek in my cabin and ask, 'Are you awake yet?'

'What time is it?'

'Nearly eight A.M. Let's have breakfast.'

Usually it was nearer to seven. Some days I'd roll over and tell him to go away. Usually, however, I'd join him for breakfast: it was a lovely time to spend alone with him, when his friends and the kids were still fast asleep.

I could have sailed like that the entire summer, but, of course, with Duke that was impossible. He loved floating along on the *Goose*, but after a few weeks he'd start to fidget and his mind would wander, and we'd know it was time to get back to the real world.

The 'real world' in this case was a special he'd agreed to do for ABC to help celebrate the hundredth anniversary of General Electric. His doctor wasn't crazy about letting him go back to work so soon, but he knew there was no stopping Duke, so he just gave him strict instructions not to overdo it. He'd have had better luck telling the tide not to come in.

The General Electric special was another one of those all-star affairs, with a huge cast ranging from Elizabeth Taylor and Henry Fonda to Lucille Ball and Michael Landon. Duke was due to work for eleven days, and though everyone was solicitous of him and the studio was amply air-conditioned, the July heat still took a toll on him. As I watched him tape, day after day, I couldn't help wishing he'd take it easy some more and not push himself so—it wasn't a very important program, after all—but Duke didn't think along those lines. From his point of view, the American Broadcasting Company had signed him to a lucrative contract, and he was obligated to give them their money's worth. He was right, of course. But was it worth getting sick over?

Unknown to me—and to anyone else—Duke had a special purpose in mind for this show. The original script ended with Duke's saying, 'Before we tie a ribbon about this beautiful evening, I want to thank General Electric for making it all possible.' On the day of the taping, Duke read off the line—but he wasn't done there. Facing the cameras squarely, he added a private little speech. 'This is the first time I have been with many of you since my recent hospital tour. So I'd like

149

to take this opportunity to thank you from the bottom of my heart for all your good wishes, telegrams, get-well cards, and your *prayers*. They came at a time when I really needed them. I wish I could thank each of you personally, but that's not possible. So I did something else. I got down on my knees and asked God to double them, and send them back to you with the gratitude of a man you've been awfully nice to for a long, long time. Thank you and good night.'

He'd finally found a way to express his appreciation. Duke never forgot a debt.

During the taping of the show, Duke had another surprise in store for me. One morning, he seemed to be acting very mysteriously, and when a couple of friends joined us for lunch, he suggested we take a drive around town. We headed down Beverly Drive, past Wilshire Boulevard, and then, without warning, stopped in front of a rather spartan brick office building. Out of the car, into the building, and up the elevator we went, all the while without a word from Duke. The elevator door opened, and we were in the private showroom of Beverly Hills' most prestigious furrier, Dicker and Dicker. Al Dicker was waiting to greet us and usher us into a small, mirrored room. He disappeared, and then returned with an entire rack of mink coats, all in my size!

'You thought I'd forgotten, didn't you?' Duke laughed, tickled to death at my confusion. My birthday had been in early June, and since Duke had been sick with the hepatitis, we'd just sort of let it slide by. It had been no big deal to me, but Duke never forgot these things.

'Go on,' he said. 'Pick any one you want. It's your present!'

'But, Duke—'

'Go on!' And that wasn't the end of it. As I was trying on different coats to make my decision, Duke noticed a beautiful white fox boa that was being brought back to the cold-storage room. He grabbed it out of the salesman's hands and instructed Al Dicker, 'here, throw this one in, too!'

'But, Duke,' I protested, 'the coat is plenty. I really—'

'It's a little hot to be wearing a coat in July,' he growled. 'I want to see you in something right now.' And then he winked. 'Come on, let your boss have a little fun.'

It was one of the loveliest gifts I've ever received in my life, made all the more wonderful by its unexpectedness.

I wore the boa just a couple of weeks later, to Duke's first major social outing after his heart surgery: a concert by Frank Sinatra at the Universal Amphitheater on July 31.

That evening sticks in my mind with dazzling clarity, for two reasons. The first was Duke's reception. Our seats were in front-row center, and as we walked down the aisle, the audience let out a thunderous roar. Everyone stood up and cheered. I was so proud it brought tears to my eyes.

Then, when Sinatra came onstage and the applause died away, he looked down at Duke and said, loudly enough for everyone to hear, 'Hi, Big Guy,' and Duke replied, 'Hi, Old Blue Eyes.' Throughout the concert, I felt as if Sinatra were directing his entire performance to us.

After the performance Sinatra bused a group of us back to Trader Vic's for dinner, but by this time Duke was beginning to fade. We waited until Sinatra arrived, and then Duke apologized and said we had to leave. Frank understood. He shook hands with Duke, then bent over and gave me a warm kiss and said, 'Thank you for taking such good care of the guy.'

Oh, how I hated to leave, but even if Duke hadn't been so tired, it would have been painful for him to stay, watching everyone drink and live it up the way he once had, and could no longer.

One by one, Duke had been deprived of his greatest pleasures in life. He had stopped going to the Big

Canyon Country Club to play cards, because all his buddies smoked, and although they told him they could forgo their cigars and pipes for the afternoon, he didn't want them to put themselves out on his behalf.

No longer could he enjoy a glass or two of his favorite Sauza Conmemorativo tequila. In the past he had been oblivious of the fact that it had an odor. Now, when I had a drink, he'd say to me, 'God, Pat, that tequila smells awful.' I thought he was resenting the fact that he couldn't have any, but one morning when a bottle fell off the shelf in the pantry, I thought, Duke's right; the stuff *reeks*.

His departure from the Sinatra party was yet another reminder that he was not the 'indestructible man,' and that all his energy had to be preserved for work, not partying.

During our drive home from Beverly Hills that night, Duke said, 'You know, Pat, I keep thinking that I'm well again. But whenever I try doing too much, I realize I'm not.' It was a rare admission for him. And it's the second reason I remember that evening so clearly.

Looking back on that final summer with Duke, I try to console myself with the fact that it was a busy, productive time for him. Besides the television shows, he made more Great Western commercials, hosted a dinner for the crown prince of Jordan—with me as the hostess!—and attended fund raisers for the Republican Party. He made the most of every day; he never felt like a useless invalid; he was always thinking of the next day, the next week, the next year. And he was always thinking of new ways of making me happy.

Although he wasn't drinking at all now, he still insisted on observing what he called our 'mystic hour,' the two of us sitting on the patio as we watched the sun set slowly beyond the bay. It was during one such twilight, shortly after Labor Day, that he broke a bit of news I had been longing to hear for years: the cottage on Bayshore Drive directly across the road from Duke's house had been vacated. I had been in love with the place from the first time I'd seen it, not least because it was so close to Duke, but discreet inquiries had revealed that its occupants were happy where they were. Now, at last, they were moving; Duke had been the first to be told of its availability— and, without saying a word, he had put down an immediate deposit.

I busied myself immediately by selling the mobile home—Duke didn't want it anymore—and getting the new place furnished. Duke gave me a pair of wonderful chests he had bought when we were in Singapore. Later, Milton Bren called and told us that he and Claire Trevor had found the perfect sofas for the place at a nearby shopping centre. By coincidence, I had seen the same sofas, but the store wouldn't sell them off the floor, and I couldn't wait six weeks for delivery. 'That's funny,' said Milton, 'they seemed so anxious to sell them to us. They promised immediate delivery and markdown if we bought both the sofa and the loveseat.' At that point Duke got into the act. He called the store, and the next morning, the sofas arrived. As with my mobile home, he threw himself enthusiastically into the role of interior decorator, buying things, arranging furniture, rendering judgements. He was like a kid with a new toy. And I was like a girl whose dream had come true. But, oh, for such a short time.

I had been settled into my home for only a few days when we were due at a banquet at the Century Plaza Hotel for the Boy Scouts of America. The Boy Scouts were giving Duke their annual award and would announce the formation of the John Wayne Outpost Camp near Lake Arrowhead in his honor. Former president Gerald Ford was also going to be on the dais—and so was I. The entrance was going to be very grand and formal: everyone on the dais filing in after the other diners had been seated, with me sandwiched in between Duke and President Ford. Naturally, the only thing I could think of was, What if I trip? In front of all those people!

Duke didn't help matters, either, when, as we pulled up to the hotel, he leaned over and said, 'Honey, be careful when you walk onstage. You know those lights are blinding. I'm used to them, but I'm kind of worried about you.' What a confidence builder.

Finally, my big moment arrived. I was on the side of the stage, and President Ford was behind me. Duke had already been introduced and was on the other side of the room. I saw the two steps in front of me and thought, I can't do it. I'll have to take them one at a time, with both feet, like a little child. God, how embarrassing. And then I remembered another thing Duke used to say when people commented on the way he walked: 'I just put one foot in front of the other.' So I put one foot in front of the other, walked out a second early so the lights wouldn't blind me, and was, thank heavens, the picture of dignity.

That evening, President Ford talked with me for what seemed like hours, mostly about Betty, who couldn't be there that night because she was in the hospital for her face-lift. I found him a warm person, easy to talk to, totally unpretentious, and still grateful to Duke for coming to his aid in the 1976 election. Because of this, President Ford, a former Eagle Scout and then honorary vice president of the Scouts, had willingly agreed to present the bronze plaque that lauded Duke 'as an example of the spirit of America and the ideals of Scouting.'

What he couldn't know was how debilitating the evening was for Duke. There were twelve hundred people present, and as usual Duke felt it necessary to put on a good show. The 'spirit of America' couldn't let on that he was totally worn out.

Worn out? The spirit of America was dying.

CHAPTER 16

EARLY in October, Duke started complaining about stomach pains. We were breakfasting on the patio and going through the mail when he pushed his plate away and said, 'I can't finish this, Pat. My stomach hurts. It feels like I'd swallowed broken glass.'

Oh, Christ, I thought, what's this? 'Maybe you should call the doctor, Duke.'

'No, no,' he said. 'I'll be all right. I don't want to bother him with every ache and pain I get.'

'Are you sure?'

'Yeah. I've got some stuff in the medicine cabinet I can take. I'll be okay.'

But he wasn't. The pains continued off and on, and he started having sleeping problems. He'd try to take a nap in the middle of the day and get to bed early, but come morning he'd tell me that he had been up during the night, saying, 'I just couldn't sleep.' He'd also dictate things into his tape recorder during the early hours, so even when he didn't complain about insomnia, I knew he had been awake during most of the night.

After a couple of weeks of this, he finally agreed to go to the doctor, and it was then that the possibility of gall-bladder surgery came up. Duke vetoed that on the spot—he didn't want to have anything more to do with hospitals just yet—but he did agree to go on a special diet that was supposed to help gall-bladder flare-ups.

On November 4 we went by private plane to Colonial Williamsburg, Viginia, where Duke was scheduled to appear on the Perry Como Christmas Special. I had urged him to cancel his commitments for the rest of the year and just stay in Newport and rest, but all he'd say was, 'Pat, I *promised* to be there.'

On our second day there the McGowans, who had been in New York, flew down to visit us, and we spent a lovely day touring Williamsburg, sightseeing and looking into the shops. Duke had never been to Williamsburg before, and the place excited him. He talked about returning the following year to do his own Christmas special there. He wanted to show America as it had been.

That night, though, he said, 'Pat, my stomach hurts again. You're going to have to take the McGowans to dinner; I just can't go. I'll have some apples sent to the room.' Duke was eating a lot of apples and watermelon then because he felt they soothed his stomach.

The next morning, he reported to work as usual, and no one suspected he was feeling ill. His weight was down to a trim 225 pounds by now, and, in fact, he looked marvelous. Privately, he said, 'I wish I felt as good as I looked.' That night, again, he made an effort to join us for dinner, but when we were almost to the restaurant, he told our driver, 'You're going to have to take me back.'

For the rest of our stay, he didn't attempt to go out to dinner again. As soon as he'd get back from taping, he'd put on his pajamas and go straight to bed.

One day I suggested casually, 'When we leave Williamsburg, instead of heading straight back to California, why don't we fly to Boston? Maybe the doctors at Massachusetts General can take a look at you'.

'No!' he replied sharply. 'I'm not going to Boston, and I don't want you to mention Mass General again!'

'Why not?' I said, and thought, What are you afraid of? But he wouldn't answer me, and so I did as he said and remained silent. With the benefit of hindsight, I know I should have screamed and yelled and *made* him agree to go, if for no other reason than to shut me up; but it was so hard to make Duke do anything if his mind was set against it. When we get back to California, I thought, I'll make sure he checks into Hoag Hospital.

But when we got back to California, he still wouldn't go. There was always some excuse, some commitment he had to honor, some meeting he had to make. His doctors urged him to go into the hospital, but he kept putting them off. 'I don't have time now.' He was in some sort of pain almost constantly by now, but it was still 'I don't have time now.' Maybe it was because he realized just how little time he had.

On December 14 we were due to leave for Shreveport, Louisiana. General Omar Bradley was going to be there, and Duke was to be presented with the Omar M. Bradley Spirit of Independence Award at the Independence Bowl, just prior to the start of a football game between Louisiana Tech and, I believe, South Carolina.

For most of the week I'd been urging Duke to cancel Shreveport. 'Let's not go,' I pleaded. 'Let's go to the hospital and find out what's happening.'

'No,' he said. 'I promised to be there and I have to be there. It'd be an insult to General Bradley.' But then—and I don't know if it was the concern in my voice or his own common sense at last—he said, 'But I'll tell you what, Pat. We'll go to Shreveport, and when we get back, I'll talk to the doctor about that gall-bladder operation. Okay? Will that satisfy you?' I nodded, relieved. 'Just don't push it,' he added.

Our host in Shreveport was Leonard Phillips, a prominent businessman, and the night we arrived, he and his wife held a small dinner party in Duke's honor, with just their children and a few close friends. Duke excused himself early, saying something about being tired after the trip, but in truth he was in such pain he just had to get into bed.

Among the Phillips' guests was a prominent

Shreveport doctor, and evidently he saw something about Duke that night that concerned him enough to follow Duke back into the bedroom. I had joined Duke by that time, and when the doctor came in, he started asking Duke some very pointed questions. What kind of pain had Duke been experiencing? When had his stomach first started bothering him? What kind of medication had he been taking? What had his own doctors said? I could see Duke trying to control his temper as the interrogation continued. And then, 'I don't want to alarm you, but have you considered that you might have cancer? The pain and all those other symptoms—have your doctors examined that possibility?'

Duke replied emphatically, 'I don't have cancer!' By now he was in an absolute fury, and he ordered the man to get out of his room. And then he turned to me and said, 'Pat, *I don't have cancer.*'

That was the first person who had actually come out and said it aloud to him: 'Have you considered that you might have cancer?' After a while Duke calmed down and shrugged. 'It's just mumbo-jumbo. He doesn't know what the hell he's talking about. Because of that lung cancer I had, it's the first thing that comes to his mind.' But he didn't return to the party, and neither did I. It was the last either of us ever saw of that doctor. In fact, I can't even recall his name.

What was wrong with us? Why didn't we call the doctor the next day and set up an appointment, question him further, ask his advice? Why didn't we? There's only one answer: we didn't want to know, so we dismissed his diagnosis as 'mumbo-jumbo.' Would a month have made any difference? It's too painful even to speculate.

Obviously he'd said nothing to the Phillipses because there was no change in their attitude the next day. Duke attended a luncheon in his honor, got through it with no difficulty, and that night our hosts took us to dinner at an Italian restaurant in Shreveport, and the conversation centred around our plans for the following day.

The best-laid plans! Duke hadn't wanted to cancel Shreveport, because he had felt it would be an insult to General Bradley. So instead the airport in Shreveport was closed by fog and Bradley's flight was canceled. Duke went to the stadium anyway, in an escorted motorcade. The crowd went wild. And then we left early, so we'd be back in Newport before dark.

The next morning, I reminded Duke of his promise to check into Hoag Hospital as soon as we were back home. 'Why not call the doctor now and book your room? We've delayed it too long already,' I said.

The mention of cancer had obviously spooked him, however, and no matter how strongly he felt about keeping his promises, he wasn't yet ready to take the fateful step.

'I'll be goddamned if I'll spend the Christmas holidays in that depressing place. What the hell is the hurry anyway? I've put up with these pains so long—I can put up with them a little longer. Now, let's get this place looking like it's Christmas.'

So out came the ornaments, and off we went looking for a tree. I could understand Duke's reluctance to spend Christmas in the hospital, but I wanted to get on with it, to find out what was really wrong, his gallbladder or . . . whatever. But he couldn't be budged. Well, if the doctors had felt it was an *emergency*, I rationalized, they'd have made him go in anyway. As long as Duke said he was going in after Christmas for sure—a couple of weeks wouldn't make that much of a difference, would it?

The week before Christmas, Duke was in a terrible mood. I'd never seen him so irritable, about practically everything, and I tried to stay out of his way as much as possible.

One day I took some time off to do some Christmas shopping for Duke and the kids with a girl friend of mine. I wanted to buy Aissa a duplicate set of make up, so she could keep a supply at her dad's house and another at her home. En route back, we were caught in a traffic jam, and it took us forty-five minutes to make it to the house.

Duke was livid when we returned so late.

'Where the hell have you been?'

'We were out shopping for you and Aissa.'

'Like hell you were. You were probably at some bar drinking it up.'

Duke knew the accusation was absurd, but he was in such pain he got upset for no reason at all. I understood he wasn't lashing out at me personally, so I did my best to ignore his outbursts.

It was difficult for us to be very merry that Christmas of 1978, not knowing what 1979 would bring. Or perhaps knowing, and fearing to face it.

The DeFrancos and the Reafsynders had been invited for dinner on both Christmas Eve and Christmas Day. Duke tried his best to be a good host Christmas Eve, but since it was obvious he wasn't feeling well, our guests left early and Duke said, 'Let's wait and open our gifts in the morning.'

I was across the road by seven A.M., but Duke had been up for hours. He still had his robe on; he just didn't feel like dressing. Ethan had stayed with a friend the night before, and didn't get there until after breakfast, which irritated Duke, and his irritation increased when we had to wait for Ethan to wrap some last-minute gifts.

Aissa, Marisa, and Ethan opened their presents first; then Duke and I started opening ours. He had bought me an elegant gold bracelet and some beautiful clothes. I gave him a Baccarat ice bucket with gold-plated handles, engraved CHRISTMAS 1978, DUKE FROM PAT, and also a five-foot-tall stuffed doll dressed in pearls and high heels. On the card I wrote, 'No fuss, no muss, no alimony, no talking back, no bother—just *a whole lot of love*—Pat.' This was my 'fun' gift, and he got a great kick out of it. But suddenly the gift-opening ceremony was too much for him. He couldn't open the rest of his presents. Instead he excused himself and went back to bed.

Michael, Patrick, and Toni all called to wish their dad a merry Christmas, and Melinda, Greg, and their children stopped by on their way to Los Angeles during the morning. The girls and I had decided to cook the dinner ourselves that night. We prepared a feast: turkey and dressing, mashed potatoes, fruit salad, a mixed-green salad, hot biscuits—everything Duke loved.

He tried to taste a bit of this and a bit of that, but it was obvious he was making the effort only to please us. He insisted we have champagne and wine with dinner, and brandy afterward, even though he couldn't even take a sip. He tried so hard to be the perfect host, and in many ways succeeded. Despite ourselves, we had a good time, which seemed to please him. He was aware how difficult he'd been. It was as if he was trying to make it up to us.

Eventually, however, he had to give in and retire to his bedroom. We all went back to my place for a nightcap, and when we looked at the clock, Christmas was over.

New Year's Day was another quiet holiday. A few friends came by, Duke watched some football and made an effort to be cheerful, and that was it. And then *finally* he kept his promise.

He had a meeting with three doctors at Hoag Hospital, and the details of the operation were finally set. It would be performed on January 12 at the UCLA Medical Center by Dr William Longmire, a specialist in the field of gastrointestinal medicine. At that point it was still gall-bladder surgery that was being discussed.

The doctors wanted to get him in sooner, but Duke still had one more commitment to keep. He had agreed to do a television interview with Barbara Walters for one of her specials, and the taping had been scheduled for the eighth. He would go into the hospital the day

161

after the interview, but not one day before.

On January 3 Barbara Walters came to Newport for preliminary talks about the taping and a tour of the house. There was an instant rapport between the two of them, and Duke began looking forward to the interview. As I've said, at this point the weight loss, though debilitating, was actually becoming to him. On his good days he even looked younger than when I had first met him. The fact that he had stopped drinking probably had something to do with it. In a way, too, the Walters special was more than just an interview to him. He was looking ahead to the time when the surgery and hospitalization would be a thing of the past, something to file and forget. He had every intention of getting back to acting. To some small degree, the special would serve as a kind of 'screen test' for him; I think he wanted to prove to himself that he could still deliver.

All that week, Duke actually seemed to be in the best of spirits. Now that the date was actually set for the operation, a cloud seemed to lift, and he began making plans for the rest of the year. For months he had been talking about moving the office out of his home, and now, suddenly, he decided that we should explore the business district of Newport for suitable space. As luck would have it, we found a perfect suite right away, just seven minutes from the house, and put down a deposit immediately. Claire Trevor Bren met me there and helped figure out which office should be Duke's, which mine, and where to place the other girls. Later Duke joined us to discuss placement of bookshelves, paintings, and so on. For a few days, at least, we had something other than the operation to think about.

He even received, or rather gave himself, a twenty-four-hour reprieve from checking into the hospital. Barbara Walters had been told nothing about Duke's imminent surgery, and late in the week her secretary called to ask if Duke would consent to tape a segment aboard the *Wild Goose*, in addition to the one planned at the house. It would require an extra afternoon, but Walters thought it would add a delightful element to the show.

'No,' I replied. 'I don't think that will be possible. I'll have to get back to you, but I don't think you should plan on it.'

When I told Duke about it, though, he said, 'Good idea. I'll do it. Call her back and tell her I'll do it. And call Bert and tell him to prepare himself for the camera crew.'

Also, I thought, call the doctors and have them call the hospital, and let everybody know that we won't be there until the tenth! Nothing would change his mind, though, and I'm certain Miss Walters would never have asked for that additional day if she had known the truth at the time. It wasn't until after the last question had been asked and the last shot completed that Duke casually mentioned he'd be going into the hospital the following day—'something to do with my gall-bladder.' It caught her quite by surprise.

Several million people watched Duke on the special when it was broadcast, on March 13, 1979. But that was so long ago. Recently Miss Walters generously sent me a transcript of that interview. I think some of it bears repeating. Even without sound and color and picture, it is so much Duke, so much the man I loved. And it was the last interview he ever gave.

BARBARA WALTERS: The day before John Wayne went into the hospital, he allowed us to interview him, I think to say what was on his mind, just in case. John Wayne has made over two hundred films; even he doesn't know the exact number. And he was the greatest box-office draw in the world for over twenty-five years . . . To all the world he is John Wayne; to his friends he is simply Duke, named, of all things, after a dog he once had. But actually he never legally changed

163

his name from the rather fancy one he was born with *[Turning to Wayne]* That's still your legal name: Michael Morrison.

WAYNE: Yes, Marion Michael Morrison.

WALTERS: You never changed—Why didn't you change it?

WAYNE: Well, what for? I can pay taxes just as well under John Wayne as I can under Marion Michael Morrison.

WALTERS: What's your idea of a very good day?

WAYNE: Well, getting up in the morning. Being still here. As far as I'm concerned I've had enough experience to know that if I open my eyes and look outside, and it's a nice, foggy day, it's great. If it's a sunny day, it's beautiful.

WALTERS: If it's any kind of a day, it's okay, huh?

WAYNE: If I'm there.

WALTERS: Are you worried?

WAYNE: Not the least bit. I'm kidding. I'm not . . . well, I'm kidding sort of on the level. No, I'm not worried. I've been around for quite a while, enjoyed the fruits of capitalism.

WALTERS: When you read now, people call you the legend, or the legendary John Wayne . . . I mean do you feel as if they're writing about a monument, or a man who isn't here anymore? Or do you say, aah, that's . . .

WAYNE: Well, yeah, that was kind of scary. Let's say, then . . . there's a thing to frighten you. They talk like you're a part of the past or something. And, rightfully so; I am a part of the past. But I also want to be a little part of the future, too.

WALTERS: Do you plan to make more films?

WAYNE: I think so, yeah.

WALTERS: Do you think you're a good actor?

WAYNE: I know I'm a good actor. *[Laughs]* But it's . . . I've been at it for fifty years. I should have learned something, you know.

WALTERS: They used to write, not just the press,

there was . . . it was kind of that there was a John Wayne-type movie, and that you always played John Wayne.

WAYNE: I try to keep myself to where they can identify with me. I remember when I was a young man and we were making a picture in which Harry Carey was playing my father. You know . . . I was imbued with the idea that I wanted to play every kind of part. And I saw Ollie Carey, that's Harry Carey's wife, sitting over there. And they loved me, and had been very nice to me. And when all these people left, she said, 'You're a big jerk.' She didn't say 'jerk,' because she used the language of the truck driver. I said, 'What's the matter?' She said, 'Look at . . .' and Harry Carey had just walked in the room and stood over there watching us. She said, 'Would you like to see Harry Carey different?' And I said, 'No, of course not!' And she said, 'Well, then, why don't you wise up? The American people have taken you to their hearts and they expect a certain thing out of you. Don't disappoint them.' [*Laughs*] And I think it's the best advice I was ever given in my life.

WALTERS: Are you you? Is John Wayne, Marion Morrison, the guy that we see on screen, is he now you? Are you rough, and tough, and a hard drinker, and soft with women, and hard with men, and . . .

WAYNE: Yeah, I think so.

WALTERS: [*Laughs*] How terrific.

WAYNE: Yeah, I like to drink. And I like women, and I've probably been a lot softer than I should be on occasion with them. And a lot tougher on some men, mainly myself.

WALTERS: Can we talk a little bit about women? I don't know whether you said this, because I went back and was reading some things from your past, but there was a quote in which you said, 'Women scare the hell out of me. I've always been afraid

165

of them.'

WAYNE: True.

WALTERS: Women scare the hell out of you? Still?

WAYNE: Yeah. I'm scared to death. [*Laughs*]

WALTERS: Why?

WAYNE: I don't know . . . you know . . . it's just . . .

WALTERS: Are you romantic?

WAYNE: Very much. Very much so. Easily hurt. Easily hurt.

WALTERS: Would you want to get married again?

WAYNE: If I were a young man of fifty or so, yes. But I think it's pretty ridiculous at seventy-one to start thinking about marriage.

WALTERS: I'll bet there is someone who wouldn't agree. You've been separated for five years.

WAYNE: Um-hmm.

WALTERS: And you separated at a time where a great many men would have said, Oh, what the heck, I'll stay with it. Is it very difficult for you, these separations?

WAYNE: I probably would've stayed with it if I thought there was any . . .

WALTERS: Hope of reconciliation?

WAYNE: . . . or any respect back and forth, you know. I just . . . it just actually . . . she's a fine woman. She's the mother of my children. We just lost contact. Completely lost contact. It's sad, in a way, but what the hell, that's what happens.

WALTERS: Yeah. Nobody ever said marriage was easy.

WAYNE: [*Chuckles*] No.

WALTERS: Is there a woman in your life now?

WAYNE: Well, I have a very deep affection for Miss Stacy. She's young and wonderful and thoughtful and has made my life very comforting. And very exciting at times. She likes to travel and likes the things that I like to do. And I have a very pleasant life with her.

WALTERS: When we talk about sexuality in pictures, or when we talk about beautiful women or sex

166

symbols . . . do you think of yourself as a sex symbol?

WAYNE: I wasn't a sex symbol but there was, I'm sure, a feeling of sex in . . . in the minds of audiences. I wasn't milk-toast in any form. So I suppose there was that . . . but, you know, I enjoyed things like in *The Quiet Man,* the relationship with Maureen O'Hara, because it was healthy and strong and it was still sensual, but it was not degrading or a . . .

WALTERS: What do you mean? What's degrading?

WAYNE: Oh, I don't know. A sweaty body and matted hair and just flesh. I mean, wet, hot flesh.

WALTERS: Yuck.

WAYNE: Yeah. It's yuck as far as . . .

WALTERS: How do you feel about doing love scenes? Wet, kissing love scenes?

WAYNE: Well, if they blocked it off enough it was a lot of fun.

WALTERS: Do you watch your old movies on television?

WAYNE: Occasionally, when there's a real oldie. Like they had *Wake of the Red Witch* on the other night. I looked at it, I don't know, till I fell asleep . . . on the late, late movie.

WALTERS: How do you feel?

WAYNE: Well, it's kind of irritating to see I was a good-looking, forty-year-old man, and suddenly, I can look over here and see this seventy-one-year-old.

WALTERS: You're not a bad-looking fellow now.

WAYNE: Well, yeah . . . but I, and I'm not squawking, but you know, it's . . . you know, you kind of think, 'God, I was pretty wonderful then.'

WALTERS: Off camera, off screen, do you like you?

WAYNE: I'm crazy about me. I just want to be around for a long time.

WALTERS: To enjoy you. At this point in your life, having faced illness, I guess having faced the prospect of death, are you, do you have a philosophy, or do you have a point of view that you think kind of sums up your thinking today?

WAYNE: Listen, I spoke to the man up there on many occasions, and I have what I've always had: deep faith that there is a Supreme Being. There has to be, you know; it's just . . . to me, that's just a normal thing, to have a kind of faith. The fact that He's let me stick around a little longer, or She's let me stick around a little longer, certainly goes great with me, and I want to hang around as long as I'm healthy and not in anybody's way.

WALTERS: Do you fear death?

WAYNE: I don't look forward to it, because, you know, I don't care what faith you have; maybe He isn't the kind of father that I've been to my children. Maybe He's a little different; maybe He won't be as nice to me as I think He will, but I think He will.

WALTERS: Has it been a good life?

WAYNE: Great for me.

WALTERS: Any regrets?

WAYNE: Great for me. Ah, here and there, probably.

WALTERS: If you had it all to do over again, would you . . .

WAYNE: I'd do it the same way.

WALTERS: The same way. Stick around for a while longer, will you?

WAYNE: I sure want to.

After the taping was done, the lighting men began taking down their lights and capping their cameras. Duke was silent as they busied themselves; then he suddenly turned to Miss Walters and said, 'Could we take that part over again where I talk about Pat?'

'I'm afraid we can't do it now,' she said. 'We have no lights, and if we set it up all over again, it might not match what we've already shot.'

Duke thought a minute and then said, 'You took pictures of Pat and me talking together, didn't you?'

'Yes', she said. 'We intended to use them in the introduction to the interview.'

'Okay, then,' Duke replied. 'When you show those pictures, would you describe Pat as my "dear companion"?'

And that's what she did. Later Miss Walters was to say that, because of that request, she 'felt even more strongly that Wayne had done an interview with us because there were some things he wanted known, some things he wanted on the record . . . just in case.'

Part IV
The Lifewatch

CHAPTER 17

DUKE checked into the UCLA Medical Center on Wednesday, January 10, at one P.M. He had stalled as long as he could. His time and commitments had run out.

Even that morning he had been fiddling around the house, trying to delay our departure until the last possible moment. I kept reminding him that we had to get going, and he kept shouting back, 'Don't rush me,' as he rechecked his suitcase to make sure he hadn't forgotten anything. He had packed a half-dozen pairs of nylon-tricot pajamas, two robes, several extra hairpieces, and some caps, so he wouldn't have to wear a hairpiece all the time.

As we left the house that morning, he was wearing gray slacks, a blue blazer, and a white sport shirt. He looked devastatingly handsome, ready for an informal luncheon party at the Balboa Bay Club. God, how we both wished that that was where we were headed!

Michael and Patrick met us at the hospital. As in Boston, they had arrived a little earlier to take care of the paperwork. The press had not yet been informed of the surgery.

I accompanied Duke to Suite 948 on the ninth floor of the Wilson Pavilion—the VIP accommodations, I suppose you could call them. Whoever had designed these facilities obviously believed in a cheerful, beautiful ambiance. The rooms were bright and sunny, and the floor contained such extras as a special kitchen and sleep-in accommodations for the patient's family, in case of emergency. I hoped we wouldn't have to use them.

Once Duke was settled in his room, I took leave of him for a little while. I had booked a room in the Holiday Inn on Wilshire Boulevard in Westwood, just two minutes from the hospital; I drove over there, unpacked, and returned to UCLA. While I had been gone, Duke had met with Dr Longmire, who had told him they planned to operate first thing Friday morning.

The following day, Thursday, the entire family came to visit. Everyone tried to be cheerful and make small talk—to hide behind the facade you usually maintain in a hospital room, when you are desperately worried.

Michael and Patrick, and Bernard Strohm, the hospital's administrator, were in charge of dealing with the press. Duke prepared the first release himself: a very matter-of-fact communiqué saying, in essence, that he was being hospitalized for minor gall-bladder surgery; that because the open-heart operation had been so successful, he was in great physical condition; that since he didn't have a movie coming up immediately, he'd decided this was the perfect time to take care of a gall-bladder problem that had been bothering him for years. The press seemed to accept it.

By six Friday morning, I was at the hospital. I wanted to be there—and have him know I was there—before the medication knocked him out. He said to me, 'Take care of Marisa if anything happens. She's the only one I'm worried about.' And then, as he was being wheeled through the door, he smiled and added, 'See you in the movies.'

By now all of Duke's family had arrived and were gathered in the ninth-floor waiting room, which had been decorated to resemble a private library. It was all wood paneled, and the walls were lined with book-shelves, though there were only two or three books per shelf. I remember wondering what had happened to the other books: had they been stolen, did the other patients have them, or had the shelves never been filled to begin with? When Duke gets back home, I said to myself, we must contribute some of our

173

books. Duke had always been a voracious reader, and we had boxes of surplus books. What a strange thing to think of! Here we were in the most luxurious pavilion of one of the world's best hospitals and I was worried about their missing books. I guess I was just trying to preoccupy my mind with something, anything except what was happening in the operating room.

The hours ticked by. Eight o'clock. Nine o'clock. Nine-thirty. I had been told that simple gall-bladder surgery lasted about two and a half hours. We hadn't heard a word.

At ten a doctor entered the waiting room. His face was impassive, but he got right to the point.

'I was sent up to tell you that Mr Wayne is still on the table. We found a cancerous stomach—and there is no option open to us except to remove the entire stomach.'

Duke had started complaining about the pains in October! It was after the fact now, the damage had been done, but I *had* to know. 'How fast does this type of cancer spread?' I asked.

'From a half inch to an inch a month.' And then, raising his hand to his chin, he added, 'But you don't worry about the rain when the water is up to here.'

Then he briskly added that Duke would be in surgery for several more hours and that he doubted we would hear anything more until the operation was over. Or . . . I'm sure we were all thinking the same thing, but none of us had the courage to ask the question. Was Duke going to die? The doctor probably wouldn't have had an answer if we had asked him. And just how many more 'several hours'? Two? Three? Four?

A little after noon, a doctor called from the operating room: surgery was still in progress. He suggested we all have some lunch. I think the girls went to the cafeteria; Michael, Patrick, and I returned to Duke's room.

Suddenly we heard Michael's name being paged on the public-address system. My heart felt as if it had

174

stopped beating. I could see the panic in Michael's and Patrick's eyes. For a moment we stood there, frozen; then Michael left to pick up the phone at the nurses' station, and Patrick blindly followed. I couldn't force myself beyond the doorway.

Michael returned in a few minutes, however, with a relieved expression on his face. He was *almost* smiling.

'That was a call to reassure us that everything is going well,' he said. 'You know, I didn't *think* when they paged me. I was too scared. It didn't occur to me that they wouldn't page us to tell us something had gone wrong. The doctors would have come up here themselves to break the news.'

Indeed, none of us was really thinking straight at that point. We simply existed from moment to moment, hour to hour. And the hours dragged by. Two o'clock. Three o'clock. Four. The girls had returned from lunch, and we were back in the library. Silence, small talk, more silence. Nobody watched television or turned on the radio or made any phone calls. We were all oblivious of what was going on about us.

Meanwhile, the situation down in the lobby was chaos. Somehow the press had learned that Duke was still on the table, and reporters had been descending on the hospital in hordes. They were all over the place. Some were claiming to be relatives of other patients, in order to get by hospital security, and a couple even put on white lab coats and made it to an anteroom behind the operating chamber before they were thrown out by security guards. None of them reached the ninth floor, but because of them, we were prisoners up there. We were advised not to leave the area; the reporters were keeping watch for members of the family.

None of us really wanted to leave anyway. Someone came in from the private kitchen and asked if she could bring up something to eat. None of us was particularly hungry, but we had to eat. I recall looking out the window and realizing that it was beginning to get dark: in January our 'mystic hour' came early. I guess we all would have welcomed a drink. Duke had been in surgery now for nearly nine and a half hours.

We were still picking at our food when the news came that the surgery had been completed. Duke was on his way to the intensive-care unit, and Dr Longmire would be up to talk to us as soon as he was free.

Every minute was an agony. We had waited nearly ten hours, and I'm sure the doctor needed some time to rest, wash up, and perhaps have a cup of coffee after such an ordeal. But I remember thinking, Where is he? What's taking him so long? Won't he ever get here?

At six-thirty Dr Longmire arrived, looking very serious and totally spent. He told us that if Duke hadn't had his heart surgery the previous March, he doubted if Duke would have survived the nine and a half hours on the table. The surgery had proceeded well, however, and Duke would be coming out of the anesthesia shortly. We'd be permitted to visit him that evening, but only one at a time and only for a very few minutes.

The doctor didn't answer the question foremost in our minds, however. The cancerous stomach had been removed, but what then?

Hesitantly, I asked a question, using a term I'd learned from all those letters Duke had written to cancer patients. 'Before you operated, had the malignancy spread? Had it metastasized?' He shook his head. We thought he meant no, definitely not, but no one could be certain until the official report was in from pathology. That wouldn't be for a couple of days.

Michael was the first to see Duke. We hadn't discussed what to tell Duke when he saw him—mindful that he'd still be thinking he'd just gone through a gall-bladder operation—and Michael seemed upset when he rejoined us.

'I can't believe what I just did. I walked over to Dad

176

and said. 'Well, you did it again!" '

We were all a little startled at that, but sympathetic. After the stress Michael had been through, the abruptness of his announcement was understandable. Besides, Duke would have wanted the truth—and, selfishly, I was relieved that I wasn't the one who would have to tell him.

The rest of the family went in to see him in shifts; I went back to the hotel and picked up a change of clothes: I had decided to spend the night in Room 948. As in Boston, I wanted to be there. If anything were to happen during the night, the doctors and nurses would know where I was. And I felt safe sleeping in Duke's hospital bed: it would be all right as long as I was there. Duke would be all right.

After the family had left that evening, I slipped into the ICU. Duke was awake and surprisingly alert. He looked at me and quietly asked, 'Cancer?' I suppose he wanted to confirm Michael's statement.

'Yes,' I replied, 'but it hasn't metastasized.'

He smiled, and a few seconds later closed his eyes and fell into a peaceful sleep.

I, too, slept well that night, my best sleep in weeks.

I woke early the next morning and went downstairs for coffee. It was then that I learned about the problems the hospital staff had been having with the press for the past twenty-four hours. Somehow I managed to evade the reporters when I left the hospital the night before. Probably I hadn't been recognized.

The reporters were still there, though, and now they had to be told something. Michael, Patrick, and Bernard Strohm held a brief press conference in which they revealed that Duke's entire stomach had been removed after the discovery of a 'low-grade tumor.' There was no evidence the cancer had spread to any other area of his body, they said.

When I arrived at the ICU, Duke was sitting up. He was attached to several tubes and monitoring devices, but he was surprisingly cheerful, and even telling jokes.

In fact, over the next twenty-four hours, his recovery was so rapid that his private nurse, Alice Day, told me the doctors felt he would be well enough to be moved from the ICU the following day, January 15, a day earlier than had been expected.

That was good news. The bad would come close on its heels, when the report came in from pathology.

On January 17, we were told that microscopic cancer cells had been found in the lymph nodes in the gastric area. The cancer *had* metastasized. Further surgery was out of the question, but we were urged not to panic: radiation treatments had done wonders in cases like this. But I was thoroughly demoralized. I had thought the worst was over, that we would just have to cope with some necessary adjustments involved in the loss of Duke's stomach, and now there was this. Radiation: even the word frightened me.

Dr Longmire told us he was going to be completely honest with Duke about this latest development, and I'm sure he was. But I guess Duke just didn't want to hear about it. When we finally got back to Newport, and Duke's doctor, Robert Egan, brought up the necessity of starting the radiation treatments, Duke protested. 'I don't have to go through that. They got it all,' he said. When Dr Egan insisted that Longmire had told Duke about it, Duke shouted, 'Well, he didn't,' and yelled for me to come into his bedroom.

'Did you know about this?'

'Yes, Duke, I knew about it. The whole family did. And Dr Longmire informed you about it, too.'

'He never told me about it! This is the first time I heard it.' Duke ended up going for the radiation treatments, but he never did admit that anyone had told him about them in the hospital.

As the news of Duke's cancer got out, the calls started coming in. They never stopped. We told most of his friends not to come by, that he couldn't see them. I wonder sometimes if we did the right thing for Duke. We felt we were doing it in his best interest. He was sick, and a sick person is in no shape to entertain. Even the intimate family constituted a crowd, but at least he didn't have to put up a façade with them.

There were exceptions. Arturo McGowan flew in from Panama, and Jack Gordean stopped by the hospital every day, not even to visit Duke, necessarily, but just to let him know he had come by. I think Pilar came to the hospital with Ethan and Marisa once, but she remained in the lobby. As in Boston, there were hundreds of flowers; people didn't know that over the past year he'd become allergic to them. The nurse would bring them to the door, show them to him, read the card, and then take them to the children's wing.

On January 18 I moved from the Holiday Inn to a small apartment at the Westwood Marquis, which I shared with Aissa and Marisa, but my life still revolved around the hospital visits. I was there by seven A.M., stayed late, went home to shower and snatch a few hours' sleep, then was up by five-thirty and back at the hospital by the time Duke awakened. I would stand with the nurse while she gave him his bath. He seemed to be happy just having me in the room with him.

Duke never ordered me to be with him so much, but it was understood that he wanted me there—and I wanted to be there. Often, after I'd left the room during the afternoon when he was asleep, he'd wake up and ask the nurse or the children, 'Where's Pat?' Even if I was just downstairs buying cigarettes or in the cafeteria, he'd ask that question. He counted on my being there.

Sometimes I'd order lunch from the hospital menu. I had that privilege, but I hated to abuse it, or possibly order anything that Duke was incapable of eating. Other times I'd grab a sandwich at the cafeteria downstairs and then have a salad when I returned home at night, or, if it was very late, order something from room service.

Marisa, Aissa, and I were compatible roommates. I

179

can recall only one instance when there was anything resembling a blow-up, and it was so damn silly. One of the girls had removed the stopper from the tub, and I couldn't find it. Usually I showered, but I had been exhausted that evening and wanted to luxuriate in a hot tub for a while—and the stopper was missing. The next day, the incident was forgotten, however. We all realized that the explosion had occurred because we were all tired, worried, and under stress. In public we were all actresses, smiling at the hospital staff and pretending everything was fine. In private, sometimes, the tension just got to be too much for us. We all understood, and forgave.

When Marisa finally had to leave to return to Newport, she wrote me the loveliest note, thanking me 'for caring for me . . . and giving me love when I need it . . . I get worried when I see the elevator door close to the ninth floor and when I think I won't see you for another few days, because I love you and I love what you have done for me and Aissa and my dad.'

If only I could have done more . . .

During the day I'd sit on a sofa in Duke's room and we'd watch TV or just talk. We had had the room adjacent to his set up as a little 'den,' since we all couldn't be with him simultaneously, and when some of the family members arrived, I usually headed for the next room to give them some privacy.

The family and I had an unspoken agreement to keep the conversation on the mild side and not to bother him with problems of any kind. Michael, Patrick, Toni, and Melinda were all additionally upset at that time, because their mother, Josephine, was also in very poor health. But I'm sure they never mentioned it to Duke. The policy was, Nothing heavy; keep it light. Maybe we kept it too light. Did we prevent him from talking about something he needed to get off his chest? Were we really doing it for him, or for ourselves?

During this slow but steady recovery period, our routine seldom varied. We talked a great deal about what was going on in the world; I'd read the letters and telegrams he had received from his friends and tell him who had stopped by to ask about him.

When he was napping, I remained in the room and read, and even started to embroider a tablecloth for the table at home where Duke and I played cards every morning. One afternoon, though, when it was time for his nap, I sneaked out of the hospital and went to a nearby beauty shop for a fast permanent, which I thought would eliminate my having to shampoo and blow-dry my hair every morning and enable me to get a little extra sleep.

When I returned to his room, he was still drowsy, but not so drowsy that when I bent down to give him a kiss, he didn't notice what I'd done right away. 'Honey, you've ruined your hair! I can't let you out of my sight for a minute!'

Aside from the times the children visited, I was rarely out of his sight. We watched a great deal of television, mainly news and game shows. 'I learn more about my condition from the evening news than I do from the doctors here,' he'd say. He was happiest with the game shows. His favourite was *Tic Tac Dough,* which came on during the supper hour, but he loved them all. In the morning he made sure to watch *Wheel of Fortune, Hollywood Squares,* and *Password;* he not only watched them but *participated,* often thinking of the answers before the contestants. I think his secret ambition was to be on one of those shows as a celebrity contestant some day.

The television news usually angered him. He'd go on tirades about the way someone in government was handling some issue or other. The stronger he got, the louder the tirade. On January 22, the press reported, 'Mr Wayne continues to improve. Vital signs are all stable.' I'd already known that. He'd had a one-way shouting match with Walter Cronkite that he'd never have been able to manage a week before!

On the twenty-fourth Duke walked as far as the

'library'—our former waiting room. It seemed like such progress! He still required assistance, however. Sometimes I would support him on one side and a nurse would on the other, or Patrick and Michael would lend a hand. Always the intravenous bottle on its metal stand rolled along behind us. The IV was Duke's constant companion for weeks. When he first got to the stage where he could go to the bathroom on his own, the IV went with him, together with a nurse. When he felt stronger, the IV still followed along, but the nurse remained outside.

Duke had had drain tubes, one on each side of his body, since the first day of his convalescence. He was so pleased when they were finally removed, but on January 25 the left one had to be reinserted: an infection had developed, which meant he'd have to stay hospitalized longer than expected. It depressed Duke enormously, but, drain tube or no drain tube, he continued with his daily walks. On January 28 he walked the entire length of the hall and back without holding on to anybody.

I thought the worst was over. Marisa and Aissa returned to Newport, and I moved into a studio at the Marquis and started counting the days until we'd be joining them there. I had no more thoughts about Duke's dying. He was getting stronger every day, sitting up more, sleeping less, and, best of all, relearning the eating process. He was even becoming interested in food again. He preferred tapioca pudding, which had always been his favorite, and became fond of an apricot-nectar drink that was extra rich and satisfying. Finally he attempted food that he actually had to chew, and was able to get it down and keep it down without trouble: such small triumphs, but so important to us both. I made a list of the new foods that pleased him most and got the recipes from the nutritionist, so that either Rosa or I could prepare them for him when he got home.

The next ten days dragged by. There was no change

in our daily routine; there were no sudden advances, no unexpected setbacks. The Arizona bull sale had had its date changed that year from Thanksgiving to February, and Duke sent a message, regretting he couldn't be there, but ending it, 'I'll be there next year.'

We were all so sure he would be. When Dr Longmire finally set D day (D for Departure) for February 10, I was ecstatic. Before returning to the Marquis, I stopped at an all-night drugstore to find a cheery card to put on Duke's breakfast tray. 'Today is the first day of the rest of your life,' it read, but I altered it to read, 'the rest of *our* lives.'

If Duke's stay at UCLA Medical Center had been turned into a movie script, I suppose this is what would have been tagged the 'happy ending.'

But one of the most painful realities I would have to accept in my nearly four decades in this world was that there is no such thing as a happy *ending*.

CHAPTER 18

ON February 10 Duke returned home. Our exit from the UCLA Medical Center had been shrouded in secrecy. We'd left by the back exit and driven to Newport in the motor home. Duke was resting comfortably in his own bed long before the press got wind of his departure.

Throughout his life, Duke had played fair with reporters, but now he had very little to say to them. We were all very careful about what we told people; even his closest friends did not get the whole story. We simply emphasized the positive: that he was walking every day, which was true, and that he was regaining his lost strength, which he wasn't.

Once again, the invitations started pouring in, and we worded his notes of regret in such a manner as to make it sound as if it were a previous commitment that kept him from accepting. This wasn't totally untrue. He had a previous commitment: he was scheduled to start a daily routine of radiation treatments.

Alice Day had returned to Newport with us. She didn't usually go home with a patient, but Dr Longmire had asked her to make an exception, and she had agreed to remain with us for a few days until things settled down.

'I'm not doing this for *you*,' she told Duke. 'I'm doing it for Dr Longmire.' None of us believed her for a minute.

During this period Duke was certain he was going to make it. We didn't talk about dying. We talked about what had to be done to readjust and 'get on with it.' As he had told Barbara Walters, he was determined to stick around a lot longer, and he was still interested in starting new projects and hopeful that he had at least one more movie left in him.

I don't think we were home more than a day or two when he decided that he and I were going to learn Spanish. He had spent months—years, really—making films in Mexico, and had been married to three Latin ladies, but he knew only a few words of the language. Now, after all these years, at the age of seventy-one, and after traumatic cancer surgery, he decided he had to learn Spanish.

I was perplexed, but I suppose, in a way, it was like the O. Henry story 'The Last Leaf.' There was a girl in the story who was very ill, but believed she'd stay alive as long as any leaves remained on the tree outside her window. A friend at last painted a leaf outside the window, so the tree would never look bare. Having a new project, something he could accomplish, something to look forward to, was in a way Duke's last leaf. And I was determined to help him keep the leaf from falling.

Ethan checked at his high school for me and came up with a Spanish teacher named Elena Montefierro. She said she had never been to a student's home before, but because it was for John Wayne, she'd make an exception. She came to the house and brought books and tapes to leave with us, so we could do our homework after she left. All his good intentions notwithstanding, however, Duke never got around to learning Spanish. He just never felt up to getting dressed and on his feet when she came. He insisted *I* continue with the lessons twice a week, though, and practice with Rosa on Sunday, and he promised that when he was feeling better, he'd catch up with me.

A few days after we returned, it was Valentine's Day. Finding a suitable gift for Duke had always presented problems. He had everything that money can buy, except, of course, for the most important thing:

185

his health. Wouldn't it be wonderful if you could call a store and say, 'Send over one package of health, please, gift-wrapped for the man I love.' But, of course, that couldn't be done, so I tried to do the next-best thing. It was typical of Duke to be worried about *my* health. Naturally, he strongly disapproved of my smoking, and although I'd go outdoors now when I lit up—he had become allergic to smoke—he said he could still smell it on me, on my hair, my breath, and my clothes.

So I decided, as my Valentine Day present to Duke, to give up smoking. I read some how-to material, and tried to psych myself into believing I really could. I planned to make a big production number of it: to wrap what remained of my carton of cigarettes in pretty Valentine's paper, find a suitable greeting, and then, with much ceremony, toss the carton into the fireplace.

Came the day, and I was so smug when I made my announcement, and so stupid! I hadn't stopped to think about what would happen when the flames in the fireplace hit the tobacco.

'What the hell are you trying to do, asphyxiate me?' Duke shouted as he staggered out of the room. I rushed to open the front door, then got the room deodorizer. The den smelled like a room that had been occupied for a month by a hundred chain-smoking politicians. Secretly, though, I think Duke was more amused than angry, even though he grumbled for days afterward that he wasn't sure which was the lesser of two evils: my smoking or my incessant talking about having *quit* smoking.

Nor did it escape Duke's attention that I was carrying an extra five pounds. When he bought me a pretty new pink dress, he noted, pointedly, that it was a size larger than usual. The not smoking may have had a bit to do with my excess weight, but my eating habits had undergone a change for yet another reason. Each night when I had dinner with Duke in his room I hoped that if I ate, he would, too. Rosa would prepare all of Duke's favorites in an effort to stimulate his appetite, and I sat there and ate all the food on my plate in order to encourage Duke to keep up with me. He had got some of his appetite back after the operation, but it was still a long way from normal.

Meanwhile, my few extra pounds became an obsession with him. I was putting on weight and he kept losing it, and he was painfully conscious of that. Once, when he had actually gained a pound, he said, teasingly, 'If I keep this up, I'll become as fat as you.' Matching my added five pounds had become a goal. He was so thrilled when he added even one fifth of that.

Although the children came to visit regularly, Pilar never joined them. I think Duke preferred it that way. They talked to each other because of the children, but that was that. Obviously, Aissa or Ethan must have told her how thin Duke was becoming, and at this she wanted to be helpful. She had opened her own restaurant and now started sending over food—a couple of vegetable soufflés and other light, nourishing meals.

Duke never tried any of them, however. One day the kids came for lunch, and Ethan said, 'Mom sent you a spinach soufflé that's simply super,' and Duke replied angrily, 'I don't care. Eat it yourself if it's so super.' He wasn't angry at Pilar for showing her concern, just terribly frustrated at his own lack of interest in any kind of food. To him, everything smelled bad or tasted rancid, but we kept lying to each other that it was a side effect of the radiation and that he'd be back on what the doctor considered a 'normal' eating pattern—small amounts of food six times a day—as soon as he was off the radiation. Looking back, though, I don't recall ever having heard Duke say, 'I'm hungry,' after his stomach had been removed.

Having no interest in food did not mean he had lost interest in living. He still wanted the mail opened and answered, and his stay at UCLA had brought another avalanche of cards and letters. Most of them were from well-wishers sending prayers and words of encouragement. Among them, too, though, were those never-ending requests for autographed pictures! Didn't they know? Of course not: we were still keeping the extent of Duke's illness as much of a secret as possible, and the announcement that he'd be at the Acadamy Awards the next month—an invitation he had insisted on accepting—seemed to minimize the seriousness of his condition, as did his appearance on the Barbara Walters show, which aired on March 13.

Anyone who had missed Miss Walters' initial comment that the interview had been taped the day *before* he had entered the hospital could have been left with the impression that Duke was still his old self. He commented on that when we watched the show, and was very pleased by the way it had all been put together. 'But I still wish I could have reshot the scene in which I talked about you, that I'd said a little more in the first place.'

'Like what?'

'Like you're my girl and I love you.'

I didn't give a damn that the whole world didn't hear that. I did, and that was all that mattered.

Lately, though, Duke's illness was making him increasingly less loving, and less lovable. The world was slipping from his grasp, and he couldn't stand it, so he would lash out in rages, sometimes over the most trivial things. I would try to weather them as best I could, because I understood their source, but sometimes I broke down, too.

One instance took place in late March. Long before I had met Duke, he had had a devoted black manservant named Hampton Scott working for him. I had heard so much about Scotty, I practically felt I knew him, though we had never met. Hearing about Duke's illness, Scotty decided to surprise him one day and come to Newport, without calling first. It didn't matter. Duke was in bed, but he was thrilled to see him and to talk about the old days.

At one point in the conversation, Scotty told me how many years he had been with Duke, and asked, in turn, how long I had had my job. I shrugged. 'Oh, only seven.' Duke's attention had been elsewere, and he hadn't heard the first part of the exchange. When Scotty left, he called me into his room and yelled, 'How dare you do that—tell Scotty he'd only worked for me for seven years? How dare you insult him that way?' I tried to explain, but Duke wasn't listening. I ran out of the room and returned to the kitchen, where I had been preparing lunch. Duke jumped out of bed and followed me there. When he entered the kitchen, I ran into the bathroom, locked the door, and cried.

At that point Aissa walked in. She told me later that Duke had tried to get her to go into the bathroom and make me come out. Aissa, of course, had no idea of what had caused the scene, but she had no intention of being caught in the middle.

I couldn't remain in the bathroom all day, but when I came out, I was still miserable. I can stand it when someone gets mad at me and then I get mad back, but Duke had hurt my feelings.

Duke was still sitting in the kitchen, waiting for me. He had calmed down by this time, and I guess something I said had penetrated. He got up, put his arms around me, told me he was sorry that he had misunderstood, and handed me a paper napkin, saying, 'Wipe those awful red eyes.'

Another nasty scene occurred over something as ridiculous as breakfast cereal. Duke had a sudden yen for Grape Nuts. Since it was pouring outside, I asked Barney if he'd mind driving to the grocery and picking up some Grape Nut *flakes*, a slip of the tongue. Rosa then prepared them in a bowl with milk and brought the breakfast tray into Duke's room. A minute later Duke yelled for me to come into the bedroom.

Pointing to his bowl, he shouted. 'This is not what I wanted!'

'But, Duke, you said you wanted Grape Nuts, and that's what it is.'

'Don't you know anything? Go get the box.'

I did, and, of course, the box said GRAPE NUT FLAKES. He took the box from me and threw it across the room. I told him there was no problem: I'd send Barney back to pick up plain Grape Nuts.

'Fine, and have Rosa remove this crap, because I'm not going to eat it.'

And so it went. But I endured it. What are those words in the marriage vows? 'For better, for worse, in sickness and in health, forsaking all others, until death us do part.' I wasn't Duke's wife, but that made little difference now. I had had the best of him: his warmth, his generosity, and his love. Now I had to endure the worst—the tempers, the moods, the sickness—aware that it might be until death did us part. I had forsaken all other men after I had become seriously involved with Duke, and I had never had any cause to worry about another woman's taking him away from me. I think I could have fought that.

Now this horrible disease was taking the man I loved from me. I couldn't fight back; all I could do was watch it as it happened, and reconcile myself to Duke's moods, knowing how much worse they were for him to cope with than they were for me.

Fortunately, Duke had a new diversion: his forthcoming appearance at the Academy Awards became his primary concern. At home he wore only loose, casual clothes. When he tried on his tuxedo, it was several sizes too large, beyond alteration, so he had to order a new one. On March 29 his barber, Alfredo, reported to the house to trim his hair. Duke really wasn't up to all this extra stress, but he felt he had an obligation to the industry. In addition, he knew that if he backed down at the last minute. it would be an admission that all the rumors were true: that his days were numbered.

Oscar night would mark his first public appearance since his operation. He was determined to convince the world that it would not be his last.

But of course it was.

CHAPTER 19

THAT Oscar night, as I described it earlier, was a triumph for Duke, but it was a horror for me when I saw those pictures afterward and realized just how sick he was.

Later, Duke prepared a statement for release to the press, but for some reason he never issued it. This is what it said:

> I would like to make one comment about the tribute of affection for me last night. It was the result of the dedication of many people. Decades of men and women who entered our business in the 20s, the 30s, the 40s, the 50s and the 60s, and brought our art form to flower by revealing intimate flashes of greatness, of nobility, of humor, of fineness of the inner soul against a growing tendency of today for realism and its vulgarities without the relief of the aforementioned beauty and respect for human dignity.
>
> Some will disparage this as Breen Office 'morality,' but I plead for guidelines of good taste, so that our peers may be proud of the product carrying the Hollywood seal, rather than have it represent an alphabetical gradation of vulgarity in our pictures.
>
> Let illusion again take the place of the hair and sweat of today. Good taste, not prudism, is my plea.

I've always regretted Duke's decision not to release

those words. It would have been a fitting valedictory.

After the excitement and stress of Oscar night, I had naïvely expected that Duke would confine his social activities to the house for a while, but I had only to look at the calendar to know that was wishful thinking. In April, 1979, Easter Sunday followed directly on the heels of Oscar Monday. I've discussed Duke's preoccupation with holidays, especially Christmas and Easter; it hadn't been diminished by illness.

The previous year he wouldn't leave for Massachusetts until after the Easter holidays. This year he decided he wanted to raise anchor and take a holiday trip to Catalina aboard the *Wild Goose*. I was scared. I knew Duke wouldn't be content to remain on the *Goose* once we reached Catalina, and he simply wasn't up to any strenuous activity.

'But, Duke,' I protested, 'I'd much rather stay home and celebrate quietly.'

'Then stay home.'

I hoped the doctors would forbid it, but Duke managed to persuade his doctor to let him skip a couple of radiation treatments, so we could have a long weekend.

Badly in need of moral support, I phoned my friend Peggy and asked her to fly in from Monroe, Louisiana, to join us. Duke wanted Ethan and Marisa along with us, too, and also invited our friends Ralph and Marjorie Wingfield. Marjorie had been fighting cancer for seven years, and Duke thought she might enjoy getting away from Arizona for the weekend.

As we pulled away from the slip in Newport, I went below deck for a while, my mind full of dark foreboding. And as I looked out the porthole, I recall thinking, This is the last time I'll ever see Catalina with Duke.

From the look in his eyes, I'm almost certain that Duke had a premonition, too, that this was his final voyage on the *Goose*. Since his operaton he had made several comments about putting the ship on the market, saying that even with the charter business it was a financial drain. I'd never known Duke worry about money; no matter how low his bank balance had been in the past, he had always had the ability to replenish it. Now, however, he had serious doubts about his ability to work again, and in spite of his medical insurance, the hospital and doctor bills were staggering, and there was no end to them in sight. Duke may have been rich in assets, but he still needed a steady income in order to keep up with expenses. Sacrificing his beloved *Goose* had become a necessity.

Once we were under way, I made an effort to enjoy the trip despite my misgivings. No worries, no doubts: gaiety was the order of the day. We dropped anchor at White's Landing and spent a quiet day aboard the *Goose*, playing gin rummy with the Wingfields and reminiscing about former times on the island—times Duke and I had shared, adventures he had had before we met. He told stories of hunting expeditions he had taken with Johnny Weissmuller, when—he said— buffalo had still roamed the island, having been abandoned by some motion-picture company that had been filming there in the early days of Hollywood. He also reminisced about John Ford, and the wild times he had spent aboard Ford's yacht with the rest of the Ford stock company—Ward Bond, Harry Carey, Victor McLaglen—weekends when none of them had drawn a sober breath. He had always been conscious of the fact that he was the last survivor of that hell-raising gang, but I can't recall his ever talking so much about Ford as he did that afternoon on the *Wild Goose*.

The next day, as I'd predicted, Duke insisted on going ashore. 'I can sit around and stare at the sea at home,' he said. We drove around the island for a while, but Duke was impatient to get to Avalon, Catalina's main town. Typically, he wanted to go shopping. There were all kinds of shops in Avalon; we had been to them many times in the past, but he wanted to browse through them again. We bought Easter cards for everyone aboard, but while I was paying for them,

Duke slipped out of the card shop unnoticed and alone. We had no idea where he had disappeared to, and I was worried sick. A half hour or so later he came back to the car, his arms loaded with boxes and bags. He had been in another store buying little gifts with which to surprise us on Easter morning.

He had overextended himself, however. We decided to skip lunch in Avalon—Duke couldn't face the sight or smell of restaurants—and headed back to the *Wild Goose*, where he retired to his stateroom for a nap. When he rejoined us later in the afternoon, I kind of hoped he'd say he was cutting the trip short and returning to Newport, but he didn't.

After breakfast on Easter Sunday, we exchanged cards, and Duke distributed the gifts he had so secretly chosen: stuffed bunnies, Easter baskets, and the like. His gift to me, one of the last I ever received from him, was two miniature bunnies locked in a hug. I still have them to this day.

Easter Sunday was bright and sunny, a perfect day to laze around and take it easy. But that wouldn't do for Duke. After the gift-giving, he announced that we would all hike across the isthmus. He needed the exercise, he said, and it wouldn't do us any harm. Exercise was very important to Duke. Before we had left Newport, he had calculated how many times he would have to walk around the upper deck in order to walk a mile a day, and even on the boat he often wore weights on his ankles and wrists to help build his strength and get some muscle tone back. But a cross-country hike? Was that a good idea? Duke would hear no objections.

We had been walking only for a few minutes when he realized that he was too weak to make it all the way across. Somehow he and Ethan found someone with a car, and they drove across. I joined him on the way back. Duke made a point of getting out of the car, walking a bit, then riding, then stopping to look at something he had seen many times before. I can't be

195

sure, I have a feeling he was going back in time again, that these places had once had a special meaning for him, and perhaps he felt he would never see them again.

He was very worn out that evening, and short-tempered, and his mood was no better the next morning, when we dropped anchor in Newport at eight. After saying good-bye to the Wingfields, who were returning to Arizona, he left the ship, got into his car, which had been left on the dock, told Barney to take care of getting Ethan, Marisa, Peggy and me back to the house, and then growled, 'I'm going to the hospital. *Alone!*'

I was stunned. I had always accompanied Duke to Hoag for his radiation treatments; he always said he hated to go alone. Knowing the way he drove, too, I was reluctant to let him go off by himself when he was in a temper. I had no choice in the matter, though, and so off he went. I attributed it to exhaustion and his increasing frustration with his failing body: if he couldn't walk across the island by himself, then, dammit, he would drive to the hospital by himself. He wanted to show me he wasn't an invalid *yet*.

But he was wrong.

Our Easter excursion to Catalina *had* been a mistake, so soon after the emotional and physical stress of Oscar night. Duke had simply pushed himself too hard, and now we were about to pay the consequences.

On the morning of April 18, I knew something was wrong when I didn't receive Duke's habitually punctual seven-o'clock call. Every morning before breakfast it was a ritual of ours to take a walk. Duke would phone and say, 'I'm on the way out. Are you ready?' And of course I always would be. I could set my clock by his call—always seven A.M. on the dot.

But this morning there was no call. When I didn't hear from him by seven-fifteen, I became nervous. At seven-thirty, I called him.

'What's wrong. Aren't you ready to go?'

196

'No, I'm not ready to go,' he replied weakly. 'I've been coughing up blood all night.'

'Duke, you're out of your mind. Why didn't you call me or Dr Egan?'

'Well, I thought maybe I'd just die.'

I told him I'd be right over, but first I called Dr Egan, who told me to call Dr John Rumsfeld and have him join us at Hoag immediately. Rumsfeld was a lung specialist who had treated Duke before.

All the way to Hoag Hospital, Duke coughed violently, a towel to his mouth. What was wrong now? Internal bleeding? Had the cancer cells invaded his one good lung? I was terrified. By the time we arrived at Hoag, Rumsfeld was awaiting us in the emergency room.

While the examination was in progress, I wandered through the hallways trying to find a pay phone. Finally, in desperation, I went into one of the empty offices and used the phone there. It was mandatory that I reach Michael. He was the oldest, the strongest, the one in the family the others called in case of emergency. He was also the one who gave the instructions.

Michael was neither at his home in Toluca Lake nor at the Beverly Hills office, but his secretary gave me a number where he could be reached. When I finally found him, I told him what had happened and urged him to get to the hospital as soon as possible. Then I returned to the emergency room. Dr Rumsfeld had completed his examination. Duke had pneumonia.

Duke was wheeled back to that familiar room on the tenth floor. Antibiotics were pumped into his veins, and an oxygen tent was made ready in case it was necessary. I was told that I had nothing to worry about: pneumonia was simple to treat, especially since Duke was in the hospital now.

After Duke had been settled in his room, I got back on the phone. I reached Aissa at the beauty shop, in the middle of having her hair colored. She had the beautician wash it out and rushed straight to the

197

hospital. I have no idea where Patrick was that day; I had left it to Michael to find him. Nor do I have any idea of how the press learned about Duke's readmittance to Hoag so quickly, but before nightfall the phone was ringing off the hook, both at the hospital and at Duke's house.

I was too upset to spar with reporters, and I wasn't certain that the other secretaries could cope, so I turned to the one person I felt could help me with the situation. I phoned Mary St John and asked, 'Can you please come down and help us?'

She arrived the next morning, went straight to Duke's house, and promptly and efficiently took charge as I shuttled from hospital to house throughout the day.

That morning there seemed to be some improvement in Duke's condition. I was again assured that the antibiotics would be effective. Naturally, the radiation treatments had been stopped because of the pneumonia, but I took it for granted that they would resume as soon as he recovered. I was concerned that their temporary suspension would cause some kind of a setback, but I kept that worry to myself. Certainly, I felt, the doctors would do nothing to put Duke's life in further danger. I was annoyed at myself for even thinking negatively, but I was tired, I was worried, and I was a nervous wreck. Consequently, my Valentine's gift to Duke went up in smoke.

On my way back from the hospital that night, I stopped and bought a pack of cigarettes and went to Duke's house to talk with Mary. She had retired for the night but had not yet gone to sleep, so we both had a couple of cigarettes as I told her about Duke's condition. Mary had quit smoking after Duke's lung-cancer operation, but that night we both needed cigarettes. 'You picked the world's worst time to try to break the habit,' she told me.

Mary had not yet been to the hospital; she thought it best to wait a few days, until he was feeling better. I tried to brace her for the shock, to warn her that she would not be seeing the same man she had known so well.

Early the next day, Ethan and Marisa came to the hospital to visit their father. He put on a wonderful show for them, insisting that pneumonia was nothing to worry about and that he'd be home in a week. The kids left happy and relieved. Later that afternoon, Michael arrived, and Duke put on an even better show for him. He didn't try to eat when Michael was there, but he acted as if he felt just great, assuring Michael, 'You don't have to worry about me; I'm okay, just fine.'

I know at that time Duke was trying to sound better than he felt for his children's sake—and he succeeded. After the doctor, Michael, and I had left Duke's room, Michael looked at me and said, 'Pat, my dad appears to be fine to me. He seems to be doing really well. I don't know why you were so worried. He's not at all as bad as you led me to believe.'

At that point, the doctor turned to Michael and said, 'Michael, the first thing you must remember is, your father is an actor.'

Duke didn't put on any acts for my benefit, however. Whatever his mood, he made no attempt to conceal it. I remained with him every day at Hoag, leaving only to return to the house to fetch something that had to be taken care of: there were certain items of mail he insisted on seeing, and even answering. We talked when he felt like talking; when he didn't, I busied myself with a book or magazine.

There were his quiet moods, and the violently angry ones. One night he smashed a bowl of tapioca pudding on the floor because he was so frustrated by his inability to eat. He was angry because the press kept reporting how sick he was, and livid when it finally came out in print that he had been having radiation treatments. Until now we had succeeded in keeping that part of his illness secret. Then he suddenly decided he hated his room. By now, April 21, he was no longer bedridden, and, walking around the tenth floor, he found an unoccupied room he thought he'd prefer. That afternoon, after we had moved him to the room of his choice, he decided he didn't like it after all and demanded to be taken back to his original one.

Most of Duke's anger was justifiable, and it was healthy for him to release it—that much I knew. It was better for him to do that than to turn it inward and fall into a deep depression. What I didn't anticipate, however, was his turning it on himself in a destructive manner. But that's what he had been planning to do.

Mary St John visited Duke on Saturday afternoon. Although I had given her advance warning about his appearance, she turned pale and let out a gasp when she saw how gaunt and wasted he had become. They spoke for a while, and she was quite shaken when she left. Duke had sensed her reaction, and after she left, his mood turned black and nasty. When I unconsciously lit a cigarette, he raged, 'Well, I knew you couldn't give up those fucking killers! Schick didn't do you any good.'

He was confused: the Schick Center in California was a habit-control center, and he had once talked Aissa into going there when she had had a weight problem. For some reason he had Aissa's weight, my smoking, and Schick all mixed up in his mind. I didn't try to correct him, though. It would have been impossible, given his mood. Instead, when I left that day, I went home and cried my eyes out. I was seized by such a lonely feeling, a profound sense of helplessness and of being forsaken.

Duke had always been such a marvelous, giving person . . . and now my sweet, generous, indestructible man was being eaten away, day by day, inch by inch. Things will be better tomorrow, I tried to assure myself. They certainly can't be any worse.

Sunday, however, he was still mad at everyone and everything. Later that day, he noticed his doctor and me having a quiet conversation and accused us of talking behind his back. 'You're telling her things you're not telling me,' he said. The doctor calmly replied, 'Duke, she's the one going home with you. She'll be with you all the time. We're merely talking about your well-being once you're home.' But Duke wouldn't be mollified.

Oddly enough, Duke had no visitors that afternoon. His friends no doubt thought that since it was Sunday, the entire family would be coming. His family, relieved that the crisis had passed, were certain he'd have an army of friends invading his room. I was the only one there—all day.

Duke seemed in no mood for idle conversation, so I busied myself by straightening out the room, sorting the various get-well cards, and making notes as to who had sent flowers, which as usual had been passed on to the children's and geriatric wards.

Duke was lying back in bed with his eyes closed, napping, I thought, when suddenly he said, 'Pat, I want you to go home and bring back my Smith & Wesson thirty-eight. I want to blow my brains out.'

I couldn't believe what I had just heard. I pretended not to hear it. I started shaking, but continued with my tasks.

'*Goddammit, are you deaf!*' Duke shouted. 'I told you I want you to get the hell home and bring my gun to me. Now, do what I tell you!'

I whirled around.

Duke's face was distorted with rage and defeat. 'Are you going to get me my gun or aren't you?'

'No'

'Then get the hell out of here, and don't bother to come back. You're no fucking use to me anymore.'

'No.' I refused to budge, but I didn't know what to do. Should I call for somebody? Try to talk sense to him? No, that wouldn't do any good. In his mood, it would probably only make things worse. But what could I do? Nothing. I would do nothing, let it blow over—I hoped. I sat down on my little chair by the window, picked up a book, and pretended to read.

That didn't stop his tirade. 'Don't you understand?' he shouted. 'I *want* to kill myself, get it over with. You'll all be better off. I'll be better off.'

I was completely unnerved, but I let him talk on, venting his anger, until, totally spent, he fell back on the pillow. Through this entire ordeal, I remained silent. I wished I had someone to run to—but who? I knew that Duke would never forgive me if I phoned Michael or Patrick. (I didn't know until weeks later that he had made the same request for his gun to Patrick the day before.) I was reluctant to tell the doctors, fearful they'd initiate a suicide watch, which would only depress Duke more. Instead I simply remained with Duke until late into the evening, and when I was certain he was asleep, I returned to my little house and another sleepless night.

The following morning when I got to the hospital, one of Duke's doctors told me that they had just performed a fiber-optic bronchoscopy on him because Duke's esophagus had been closing up, a side effect, apparently, of the radiation. It was one of the reasons he'd had trouble eating. The results were encouraging, the doctor said, and, barring complications, Duke would be discharged the following Wednesday. I was glad to hear that, but still, this sudden operation came as a bit of a shock to me. And I was still scared from the day before. I said, 'You know, Duke has been awfully depressed, and there are an awful lot of guns in the house. What if he becomes careless with them?'

The doctor obviously felt I was dramatizing, and smiled tolerantly.

'Oh, I don't think he will. But there's nothing that can be done about that, is there?'

Of course, there *was* something that could have been done. I could have packed Duke's gun collection off to storage, but if I had, Duke surely would have noticed, and, again, it would only have depressed him more. Then I rationalized that it was the aura of death pervading the hospital that was causing his suicidal mood. I thought, once we get home, he won't harm himself, not with the children coming in and out all day, not with little Marisa around. I never mentioned that Sunday afternoon to Duke, and he never brought it up again.

On Wednesday, with no fanfare, we returned to Bayshore Drive. A few hours later Dr Shapiro, Duke's radiologist, dropped by to make the 'tattoo'—the permanent mark that indicated where future radiation treatment would be centered. Dr Shapiro didn't stay long. As I walked him to the door, he mentioned he had to rush off, since it was Secretary's Day and he had to take his secretary out to lunch. I asked if he had an idea when Duke would be scheduled for radiation again. He just shook his head and muttered, almost to himself, 'It doesn't seem to be doing any good anyway.'

I didn't want to hear that. I had been having my own doubts about the effectiveness of the radiation, but for the first time my feelings were being confirmed. I had planned to tease Duke about the tattoo, to feign disappointment that Dr Shapiro hadn't etched a heart with our initials on it around the mark. Now I just wanted to block the entire subject from my mind.

When I returned to Duke's room, I said cheerfully, 'Hey, did you know it's Secretary's Day?'

'Yeah, I know,' he said, as if he didn't care.

Fifteen minutes later, a delivery truck from Morrie's Flowers pulled up to the house, and a boy handed me the most beautiful bouquet of spring flowers I'd ever seen. I thought they were for Duke, a welcome home gift from one of his friends, but they were for me—from Duke. I rushed back to the bedroom and asked stupidly, 'Who did this?' because I usually ordered all the flowers.

'Who do you think did it? While you were out of the room this morning at the hospital getting me checked out, I called Morrie's. I'm still capable of making my own phone calls.'

203

As sick as he was, he'd remembered how sentimental I was about Secretary's Day, because it was my job that had brought us together. Though our relationship had progressed far beyond that of secretary and boss, Secretary's Day had continued to mean something special to me, and though I had forgotten all about it this year, Duke hadn't. I think, too, the flowers were Duke's way of apologizing, of saying, 'You're still my girl.'

Now that he was home, Duke had one other thing to get off his chest. He had been enraged by the press reports of his illness, some so highly exaggerated as to have him at death's door, and before he settled down to his nap, he wanted to respond. 'I haven't lied to the press about anything,' the statement he issued that afternoon said. 'But they will not take our reports as truthful. They sneak around trying to bribe people to say something that *won't* coincide with the official report. I don't know why it is necessary, but I guess that is modern-day "news methods." It used to be considered "yellow journalism." Anyway have a happy day. JOHN WAYNE.'

But, of course, Duke *had* lied to the press, or at best told half truths. We had *all* lied or fed half truths to the press, to our friends, and to ourselves. How could we do otherwise?

CHAPTER 20

OBEDIENTLY, Duke remained in bed throughout the afternoon and evening, but he found it difficult to eat the meals Rosa prepared. Friends who had called Hoag to inquire about his condition and been told that he had been discharged automatically dialed the house. Duke had an unlisted number, of course, but so many people were privy to it that we might as well have advertised it in the Yellow Pages. Pulling the plug in his room didn't help, either. When he was awake, he could hear the ringing in the other parts of the house, and he had to know immediately who was on the line.

Why don't they all leave us alone? I kept thinking. Don't they know how ill he is? I can't take this anymore!

Finally, risking Duke's anger, I decided to tell all callers that he could neither see nor speak to anyone that first day home. He was resting: doctor's orders. I also tried to discourage anyone who wanted to visit the following day. We had been looking forward to Maureen O'Hara's visit on the twenty-seventh. We hadn't seen her since our 1977 trip to St Croix, and I wanted Duke to be strong enough to enjoy her.

I spent the night at Duke's house, in case he needed anything. The next morning, his dietitian arrived with a liquid diet that had been especially prepared for Duke. At Hoag, Duke had refused intravenous feeding, but he promised to drink this formula to help him gain back his weight. The dietitian had no sooner left than Harry Jackson, who'd created some celebrated bronzes of Duke, arrived at the house with his wife, Tina, and their son Jesse, who was Duke's godson.

205

Before Duke had been hospitalized, Harry had been talking about doing a bronze bust of him, and wanted to discuss it further. He'd called that morning, and, to my dismay, Duke had invited him to the house.

I don't think Duke had expected Tina and Jesse, too, but when he learned they were along, he forced himself out of bed to greet them in the den. I loved Harry and Tina, but I resented their visit. I guess I resented anyone or anything that was a drain on Duke's energy. And Duke loved little Jesse, who couldn't have been more than two years old at the time, but when the baby started playing with the television knob on the set in the den, Duke lost patience, and hollered, 'Dammit, can't you leave that alone!' Little Jesse was so frightened he began to cry, and Duke seemed bewildered that he could behave that way to a baby.

The Jacksons remained another hour or so. Duke was interested in the idea of the bust, but he finally had to explain to Harry and Tina that he had to get back into bed.

Maureen O'Hara arrived, as scheduled, early the next afternoon. She had been in Los Angeles for her annual medical checkup and as usual was using her brief visit to the States to visit her dear friends and relatives. Lovely, wonderful Maureen. She had had her own share of sorrows—the year before, her husband, Charlie Blair, had died in a freak plane accident—but when she swept into Duke's den, she was bursting with wit and gaiety and nonstop conversation.

En route to the house, apparently, she had been ordered to pull over to the curb by one of Newport's finest.

'Did he want to know how fast I was going?' asked Maureen. 'Of course not. Had I passed a red light or made a U turn? Don't be silly. I was doing absolutely nothing wrong. Then why was I told to pull over to the curb? That policeman recognized me and wanted to know if I was in Newport to visit John Wayne. I told him I didn't see how that was any of his concern.

206

But before I could put my foot on the brakes, he whipped out, his traffic book, handed me a pen, and asked for my autograph! The nerve of that lad!'

The story loses something on the printed page, but the way Maureen told it, complete with dialect and gestures, was all the tonic Duke needed. For the first time in months, he was roaring with laughter.

Maureen had planned to stay the day and leave that night; she had other engagements in town. Instead, she broke them and stayed for three days, and no matter that she had only the clothes on her back. Because Maureen was five foot eight to my five-three, I couldn't lend her anything of mine, but it didn't seem to matter. Rosa laundered her clothes every night, and every morning Duke would tell her how pretty she looked—commenting on her brand-new outfit. It became a private joke between them.

Throughout her stay, Maureen put on a cheerful Irish act with Duke. At no time did she let on how seriously worried she was about him. I never met a gal who could talk as much as Maureen, and tell such funny tales. There was happy banter all the time she was there. They had shared so many happy times. Duke later said that he recalled some of the stories differently. 'But, what the hell, she makes them *sound* better,' he added.

Maureen reminded him of the time in 1977 in St Croix when she'd dutifully asked what he'd like for dinner, and he'd replied, 'Steak.' And the next night, again, 'Steak,' and every time she'd tried to entice him with some wonderful new island dish she had discovered, he'd just shake his head and say, 'Steak.'

We all laughed about that, but when we were alone, Maureen was devastated. 'Heaven forgive me, Pat, I just wasn't thinking.' In her efforts to amuse Duke, she'd forgotten that it was now impossible for him to eat steak. There were tears in her eyes when she told me, 'Pat, just a couple of years ago, we were all so happy when we were together. Now Charlie is gone and Duke is so sick.'

We talked a great deal about how she was coping with the loss of her beloved husband, the man who had made her far happier than her career ever had. It had been a cruel irony that she had been at their summer home in Ireland when his plane had gone down in St Croix. Duke had been too ill to attend the funeral but had called Senator Barry Goldwater to help her get Charlie buried in Arlington National Cemetery.

Duke kept trying to be a good host; he would walk out onto the patio to talk with us. At one point he mentioned that he'd be celebrating—'if you want to call it that'—his seventy-second birthday the following month and Maureen refused to be sympathetic. 'So what? I'll be fifty-eight in August. Age doesn't matter. The mileage never hurt a Rolls-Royce. We are a couple of Rolls-Royces!'

Duke loved that, but when he left us and returned to his room, Maureen and I exchanged looks that said it all.

Maureen stayed until Sunday afternoon. She knew when she left that she would never see Duke again, but when she said her good-byes, she included an invitation to visit her in the islands soon—both of us.

Maureen was leaving, but our visitor's day was not over. As Maureen walked through the patio toward the driveway, Milton and Claire Trevor Bren arrived. The Brens had Milton's nurse with them. Milton, too, had just got out of the hospital. He was suffering from a malignant brain tumor. It was so sad, so touching —this reunion that was, in reality, a farewell.

I remember that visit vividly, too vividly. Milton was wearing a straw hat over his bandaged head, and he and Claire were wearing jogging suits. By coincidence, Duke, too, had on his jogging suit, the same color. No one planned to go jogging that day, however. The suits were to conceal the men's alarming thinness.

Milton and Duke were 'wearing' something else identical as well: that chilling tattoo, the unmistakable mark of a patient undergoing radiation treatment. Milton's was on his head, he told us; Duke's, on his chest. I can't say whether Duke was more shocked at the sight of Milton or the other way around, but on that afternoon they made a pathetic attempt at humor.

'Look at us,' Duke kidded. 'Aren't we a sight for sore eyes? The great American athletes.' The sad thing is that they had been so athletic and had done so many things together. Milton had been a terrific sailor, and he and Duke had had such great times, fishing and sailing, long before I came into Duke's life.

Remembering the good times, Milton said lightly, 'Well, we can't do it all over again.' But from the look on their faces you knew how much they wished they could.

His nurse had to help Milton to the sofa. Claire sat on the arm of the sofa, but we let the men do all the talking. We didn't have to talk; as with Maureen, when our eyes met, that said it all. Our men were on borrowed time.

The Brens stayed for about half an hour. Neither Duke nor Milton wanted to break it up so soon, but neither had the energy for a prolonged visit. Duke hugged Claire and shook Milton's hand. There were no jocular, 'See you soons.' No dramatic parting words either: just a simple, 'Take care of yourself.'

That was the last time Duke saw the Brens. Milton died the following December.

Duke retired to his bedroom for a nap. I went out to the patio to smoke a cigarette and fortify myself with a glass of wine. I didn't want to think about Charlie Blair or Milt or Duke, but I had no control over my thoughts or emotions that afternoon.

Who was better off? I wondered. Charlie, killed instantly, with no fear or suffering? Or Duke or Milton, living day after agonizing day, but with just enough hope that perhaps some miracle might happen?

And of their women, who was the luckiest? Maureen,

209

who had been subjected to that one piercing shock of discovery that the man she worshiped had died without warning? Or Claire and myself, helplessly observing the daily deterioration of our men, suffering in our own way almost as much? At least, I thought, we've had time—time to prepare ourselves, to treasure every moment we had left with our loved ones.

I shook it off. I couldn't be morbid. I forced myself to be cheerful, and to adopt a business-as-usual style for Duke's sake in the days that followed. And it was 'business as usual' for him, too. Remarkably, he was still considering the possibility of doing *Beau John*, and he invited Yakima Canutt, the great stunt coordinator, to the house to discuss some ideas he had for future Great Western commercials.

Physically, however, Duke seemed to be melting away. With the exception of an occasional 'good day,' there was little sign of improvement. Once more, we were living one day at a time.

There was only a month left of the life watch.

CHAPTER 21

IT happened during the 'mystic hour' the Tuesday following Claire's visit.

I was on the patio, just outside Duke's bedroom door, having a glass of wine; Marisa and Aissa were in their room watching television. Duke, I thought, was napping, after a futile attempt at trying to eat a little something from the tray Rosa had brought into his room.

Suddenly I heard Duke's voice calling me into his darkened room. I couldn't see his face, but I heard his words clearly: 'Pat, I have got to go to the hospital. I'm in such pain. *I have got to go to the hospital.*' He stumbled around, trying to get dressed, refusing my help but telling me to get in touch with Dr Egan, so he'd be expected. Just before we were to leave the house, he went into the girls' room and said, 'Pat and I are going to Hoag. Don't you want to go with us?' He was so matter-of-fact about it that Marisa and Aissa, believing it was just another routine visit, replied, 'No, we'll just wait here.'

I drove Duke to Hoag in his car, as slowly and carefully as I could, but in his condition every tiny bump was agony, and he kept yelling, 'Can't you slow down? You're hitting every bump! You're killing me!' The five-minute drive seemed endless.

Dr Egan met us in the emergency room at Hoag. He and Duke exchanged a few words, and then Duke was placed on a small metal bed and rushed into the X-ray room. The X-rays were processed in record time and carefully studies. I was in the room at the time, and although Dr Egan maintained a professional demeanor, he was obviously quite disturbed by what showed up on the plates. Certainly he was not evasive.

'There is an intestinal blockage there, and since this is Dr Longmire's case, I think we better call him and get you to UCLA immediately.'

Dr Longmire was out, and his assistant who had worked on Duke's case in January had been assigned to another hospital.

In desperation I told the girl on the switchboard, 'This is John Wayne's secretary. It is urgent I speak to Dr Longmire at once,' and I left the extension number of Hoag's emergency room. I told Duke I wanted to telephone his daughters as well and prepare them for the trip to UCLA, but he said, 'They didn't want to come here with us. Why do you want to call them?' I explained to him that they hadn't been aware of the seriousness of the setback, since they'd been through so many false alarms, and that it was unreasonable of him to feel hurt.

'Okay,' he said, 'call them. And call the boys.'

I did so, and then rushed back to the house to pick up some things for Duke and myself. By the time I arrived there, the girls had got in touch with Ethan, who rushed off to Hoag to drive Duke and me into Los Angeles. The girls, of course, insisted on going straight to UCLA in Aissa's car. Now that they knew the truth about their dad's condition, they were devastated that they had been so matter-of-fact about his request that they join him at Hoag.

From the moment Duke was told that he had to return to UCLA, he rejected the idea of going by ambulance. No—Ethan would drive the station wagon. He permitted some staff members at Hoag to outfit the station wagon with sheets, blankets, and pillows, so that at least he could be prone during the long drive.

Dr Longmire had returned our call while I was at the house. He told Duke his old room was vacant and

212

would be prepared for him, and to come straight to the emergency entrance. Duke had insisted on complete secrecy, which, of course, was promised. While we were still on the freeway, however, the secret was broadcast to the world on one of the local television stations. We never discovered who the informer had been, but Michael later told me he had received a call from the television station only minutes after I had spoken to him, with the report that his father was on the way to the UCLA Medical Center.

By the time we arrived, there was a battery of television cameramen and newspaper photographers waiting outside the hospital. I guess they thought it was important to show him in that horrible condition to television viewers. We evaded them by driving to the back of the hospital, and the security guard there recognized Duke immediately and got us into the hospital and up to the ninth floor without anyone seeing.

Dr Longmire came by and informed Duke they were going to do a little checking and then decide what course to take regarding the blockage. Duke was also told that he'd be put on an intravenous solution. Unlike at Hoag, this time there was no argument.

Because Duke had slept most of the day, he wanted to stay up and watch the Johnny Carson show, and wanted me to stay with him a while. The girls had already booked rooms for us at the Holiday Inn on Wilshire—the only vacancies in the area. 'I can use a good laugh at this point,' he told me. And he *had* a good laugh. I remember that Carson was doing his 'Floyd R. Turbo' routine—that character in the plaid shirt and woodsman's cap whose views were somewhat to the right of Attila the Hun. Duke roared whenever Carson did Turbo—because he felt that was the way his own superliberal adversaries wanted to picture him. I wonder whether Johnny Carson ever found out that he was responsible for helping Duke get through some of the most agonizing nights of his life.

I left Duke about twelve-thirty A.M. but was back at the hospital by seven the next morning, only to be told that they were preparing Duke for surgery. There was no alternative. Those months of sickening radiation had been useless. The monstrous cancer cells had resisted every attempt to destroy or contain them.

I was asked to sign a form giving permission for the operation. Since no one else was there at the time, I signed, and then called Michael immediately to let him know. He in turn called Patrick, Melinda, and Toni, and I awoke Aissa, Marisa, and Ethan back at the Holiday Inn.

Duke was wheeled into surgery at about eight-thirty. Later I learned he had told one of the doctors, 'Well, here I am. We have to try. Pat and my kids have talked me out of shooting myself.' By ten-thirty, with the children all at the hospital by now, we got word that everything was 'going all right.' Another hour or so later, Duke was wheeled out and taken to the intensive-care unit.

Since I wouldn't be able to see him until he regained consciousness, I took advantage of the time to move into the closer Marquis, along with the girls, and then rushed back to the hospital, where I was allowed into the ICU for a few minutes. Conversation was out of the question. I just wanted him to know I was there.

I think it was Dr Longmire who told me that Duke's heart was in wonderful condition, and that it was because of that fact that the day's operation had gone so well. The words kept going through my head: 'The operation was a success, but the patient died.' The patient hadn't died, but in my emotional state I kept thinking, Why, if there is a God, did He let Duke survive that heart surgery only to subject him to the nine-hour stomach removal, and now this? If it hadn't been for the good heart, he would have been spared those months of suffering. No one should have to suffer as he was. What kind of God was He to make this man suffer so? Why? I almost understood why Duke had asked me to bring him his gun.

I had a great many morbid thoughts that day and night of May 2, but I tried to pull myself together, to be bright and cheery when I visited Duke again the next morning.

When I saw him on May 3, he was very alert.

After he asked if I was *sure* that I had canceled whatever commitments he had made for the next few weeks—he was still concerned about letting people down—he told me that he'd be back in Room 948 later that afternoon. He seemed quite pleased about that, and added, 'I'll be able to turn on the evening news and find out how I'm doing.'

Once Duke was resettled in 948, however, he had no intention of waiting for the evening news. A few minutes after I entered his room, he asked me, in a very quiet voice, 'Bad news?'

There was a look of hope in his eyes, one that almost beseeched me to say no.

But I had to be honest. 'We don't know yet.'

Then he said, 'If I can't get well, I just want to die.'

'Duke,' I replied, 'I just want you to get well.'

'Me, too. But if I can't, I want to die.'

Innocuous releases went out to the news media. A few pesky reporters tried again to get onto Duke's floor, and failed. There was a guard outside and a NO VISITORS sign posted on Duke's door. The only visitors were to be his family and myself.

On May 5 an additional visitor was allowed.

President Carter was in Los Angeles for a local celebration and had requested permission to pay a call on Duke, if Duke was up to seeing him. We alerted Duke to expect President Carter, and the president in turn was alerted to the seriousness of Duke's condition and asked to keep the visit brief.

President Carter remained in Duke's room alone for maybe five minutes, then came out and asked his nurse, 'Is he a good patient?' Afterward he joined us in the adjacent room for a few moments of optimistic conversation, and to have a picture taken with us. (I don't know who set that up.) He never once asked, 'What's the story?' or any leading questions.

Once again, the deluge of get-well wishes started pouring in. This time we were prepared, and had the mail forwarded to Newport, but after nearly seven years of devoted attention to the mail, I could no longer care about it. All my concentration was on what was happening to Duke—and, to be honest about it, what my life would be if the unthinkable became a reality.

On May 6 Duke received a cable from the writer Robert Parrish, who was in London at the time. It read, 'Dear Duke: Among many others throughout the world, my heart is with you. BOB PARRISH.'

Duke insisted on dictating an immediate reply: 'Dear Bobby: Your thoughtfulness was very much appreciated. The further out you go, the lonelier it gets. Affectionately, DUKE.'

I decided not to send it. I didn't know where it would end up. I didn't want anybody to find out how serious Duke thought his condition was. I told Michael about it, and he agreed with me. It was the first time Duke had told me to do something related to my job and I had refused to follow his instructions. But Duke's words still haunt me: 'The further out you go, the lonelier it gets.'

On May 7 we were told that Duke could drink some fluids. He also walked a little that day, and he was even gaining a little weight because of the medication in the IV. He was so thrilled as he looked at the scale, but when he got up and glanced at his image in the mirror, he said, 'Look at me. No muscle tone.' This man had had such a beautiful body, and there was no muscle tone left. But what did that matter? As long as he was gaining weight, there was hope. That was the important thing.

The following day, though, most of our hope was

shattered.

Dr Longmire gave us the intolerable news: the cancer had metastasized. It was all over his body. His operation had been merely an intestinal bypass, the blockage would undoubtedly recur, since the cancerous cells were still multiplying.

We were also told that although doctors sometimes left a waste bag outside the body after this kind of operation, in this case they hadn't. They felt it would have been abhorrent to Duke. Now they were waiting to see if 'normal' bodily functions would begin again. And they were considering administering immunology treatments.

Dr Longmire's news was extremely depressing. We knew everything possible was being done for Duke, but to what avail? How long would he live? The doctor didn't know.

Duke felt strong enough to see visitors the afternoon of May 8. Jimmy Stewart and producer Paul Keyes came by, and I went into the adjacent room so Duke could speak privately with his friends. I have no idea what they talked about, but I could imagine it: 'You'll be up and about in no time.' 'Don't let this get you down.' Small talk. Performances on everyone's part.

I knew. I was learning to master the art of small talk, of acting a role, and I played my part to the best of my ability. I didn't break down—oh, sometimes alone in my hotel room, but never where it would matter, where anyone else would see.

I could say, 'Duke is not having as good a day as he had yesterday,' and make it seem as if it wasn't really that bad, even when his old friends called. They'd spill their feelings out to me, and I'd keep my emotions intact. The only alternative would have been not to talk to anyone, and Duke wouldn't have wanted that, so I controlled myself, met and smiled and talked and said nothing, not even to Joe DeFranco, Jack Gordean, or any of the other members of the inner circle who were at the hospital just about every day. They'd see him if he was feeling up to it; if not, they just wanted him to know they were out there.

On May 10 Frank Sinatra and his wife Barbara came to visit. When they came out of Duke's room, there were tears in their eyes. Aissa had told them that Duke had put on some weight and looked 'just great,' so they hadn't been aware of his condition until they had come face to face with it. Barbara came over to me and said, 'Pat, I was so shocked, I didn't know what I was saying. Will you please tell Duke I was a little confused and didn't say what I meant? I told him that I'd pray to St Jude for him—and that's the saint of lost causes. I meant to say I'd pray to the saint of hope. Please tell him that.'

When I returned to Duke's room, however, he didn't seem to be aware of the mistake. He had been so touched by their genuine concern that he'd heard only that she'd be praying for him.

On Friday, Duke began immunotherapy. This process was still fairly experimental, and its success had really been with people who had a minimal amount of cancer, but the doctors thought it was worth trying. The idea was to stimulate the body's immune system so that it would fight against the cancer itself, which involved repeated injections of chemical extracts into the body. One day the needle would be injected between the fingers, the next between the toes. It was not horribly painful, but it was painful enough.

Still, Duke didn't complain. He submitted without protest. I remembered the countless other times he had been hospitalized, his anger, frustration, and complaints. Now he was almost pathetically docile— and yet he wasn't giving up. He was still trying. Even after that first immunotherapy treatment, he insisted on walking the length of the hall. He didn't want to be confined to his bed or to his room. That day, I walked alongside him, with Alice Day on the other side and his IV trailing behind on a metal cart. There was the usual traffic, with the usual question: 'How are you today?' Duke's cheerful reply would be 'I'm doing just great.' He was trying so hard, being so brave.

Around-the-clock nursing was arranged; the entire family—with the exception of Ethan, who had to catch up on his grades at school—was at the hospital every day. When they were with him, I took the opportunity to dash down to the cafeteria for some coffee or to the library for a cigarette, but it seemed I never left the room without Duke's asking, 'Where's Pat?' He seemed so happy when I told him I had found a popcorn machine in the cafeteria, which worked by microwave. He knew I loved popcorn and thought it great that I had found one of my favorite foods downstairs. In the evening, when everyone had gone, I'd remain in his room, reading when he didn't feel like talking, and watching the evening news with him. He still argued with Walter Cronkite, and still tried to remain awake for the Carson show.

When I arrived early on the morning of May 13, I could sense something was terribly wrong from the way Duke looked. He made no attempt to conceal his distress. 'Last night was the worst yet, Pat,' he told me. 'The worst night ever.' He didn't want to elaborate. I later learned that he had been spitting up bile violently and without let-up throughout the night. Even though he was feeling weak and miserable, he still insisted on walking a short distance that day. I kept thinking, These damn walks are crucifying him. But he wouldn't give up, so I said nothing.

The following day, Michael asked, 'Do you know who Father McGrath is? He's in the lobby and wants to see Dad.'

I told him I did know him. Actually, he was Archbishop Mark McGrath, from Panama. He was the brother of Eugene and Robert McGrath, old friends of Duke's, and we had met him on a trip to Panama we had made the year before.

Duke hadn't walked that day—hadn't felt like it—but

he got out of bed and was sitting in a chair when the archbishop entered the room. I left, to give them privacy, and so I don't know what they talked about. What I do know is that sometime during those last few weeks, Duke made peace with his Maker. He had always said that if he were going to have any one religion, he would be a Catholic. He had married his first wife, Josephine, in a Catholic ceremony, and their four children were Catholics. Now, because Josephine had been granted a papal dissolution of their marriage and Duke's second wife, Chata, was no longer alive, it was possible for Duke to be received into the Catholic Church. And that is what happened. When Duke died, he died a Catholic.

On May 15 I left the hospital to lunch with Pilar at the Westwood Marquis so she could sign the papers that stipulated Michael would be in charge of all arrangements if and when Duke died. It was a difficult meeting for both of us. How could it be otherwise? Pilar knew how things were with Duke; her children had kept her informed, and there was nothing I could add. I wondered if she felt hurt that Duke hadn't asked to see her, but she never mentioned it; nor did she comment on Duke's relationship with me. We kept the conversation light, but an underlying sadness pervaded the meal.

There were many other papers that had to be signed that week as well. Before he had returned to the Medical Center, Duke had indeed put the *Wild Goose* up for sale, and a lawyer had bought it for a bargain-basement price. I'll never forget the heartbreak in Duke's eyes as he placed a straggly signature on the bill of sale. Another ending.

In spite of the immunotherapy, Duke was losing ground. On May 17 Dr Longmire was forced to admit, 'He is slowly declining,' and a nurse removed the scale from his room. There had been no further weight gain, and the hospital didn't think it wise to have the scale around to remind him. On May 18, though, he still managed to walk with Patrick and Michael as far as the nurses' station, a short distance from his room, and he was still very alert. I remember standing in the doorway of his room as they returned and his saying, 'Aren't you wearing the same dress that you had on yesterday?' Actually, I had been wearing a reversible outfit he had bought for me at Amen Wardy's in Newport, and I had worn it the day before, but with the other side out. I thought it made little difference, but he noticed it and he cared. How I looked still meant something to him. As far as I was concerned I would have been happy to throw on anything at hand and get myself to the hospital, but if I had let myself run down, he would have taken it as a sign that I had lost all hope, and I couldn't allow that to happen. One day I arrived at the hospital without a gold bracelet he had given me, and he immediately wanted to know why I wasn't wearing it. When I reluctantly admitted that I had misplaced it, and couldn't find it, he insisted I keep looking. Each day, he'd look at my arm and ask, 'Haven't you found it yet?' It really mattered to him. He was dying, and it mattered that I find my bracelet.

On May 19, he called before I left the hotel and asked me to pick up a couple of cool-water humidifiers to put in his room. He was having trouble breathing. That day, too, I remember standing in the doorway between the two rooms and watching Melinda help her father get out of bed to go to the bathroom. He was standing in the middle of the room, she holding on to him. She looked up at him and he down at her, and I saw his eyes fill with tears. They looked at each other, saying nothing, but I knew Duke was thinking, Have I come to this: that my daughter has to help me go to the bathroom? No words had to be said. It was all in the eyes.

Meanwhile, Duke's seventy-second birthday was coming up. Oh, how we wanted to make May 26 a happy day for him. We all went shopping for cheerful gifts and hid them away in the closet of the adjacent room. Melinda bought some beautiful sheets for his hospital bed, so he'd have something softer and more comfortable than the fuzzy thing on which he was sleeping. Before he had been hospitalized, I had thought about sending for some gold-plated barbells I had seen in a Neiman-Marcus catalogue—a fun gift, and practical, then—but now that was out of the question. Then I noticed a robot-type thing in a local toystore window. You pushed a button and it asked a question; then you had to punch in the right answer. It was a silly thing, but I thought he'd have fun with it, because he loved his game shows so much.

Another present was in store for him as well—a magnificent one.

A few weeks before, Barry Goldwater had introduced a bill in Congress to authorize the minting of a special gold medal as a tribute to Duke. Only eighty-seven people or groups had been so honored since the medal's inception, in 1776, including George Washington, John Paul Jones, the Wright brothers, Thomas Edison, Charles Lindbergh, Irving Berlin, Bob Hope, and Robert Kennedy.

On May 23 the hearings finally took place in Washington, D.C. Maureen O'Hara flew in to appear on Duke's behalf; Elizabeth Taylor, who was now living in Washington as Senator John Warner's wife, spoke eloquently; and other friends who could not make it to Washington wired their testimonies. Barry Goldwater read many of them out on the Senate floor and inserted others into the *Congressional Record*—sentiments from Frank Sinatra, James Stewart, Gregory Peck, Kirk Douglas, Jack Lemmon, and, of course, Katharine Hepburn. So many thousands of words of praise and acclaim and love were read that day, but the briefest statement—Miss Hepburn's—summed them up perfectly: 'I understand that the United States Congress and our president are giving John Wayne a gold medal. Asked for a comment, I can only say, with a heart full of love for all concerned, "About time." '

The bill was passed, unanimously. On one side the medal would bear a portrait of Duke as Davy Crockett in *The Alamo;* on the other side, a landscape of Monument Valley. The inscription—as proposed at the hearings by Maureen O'Hara—would read, simply, 'John Wayne, American.'

Duke was awfully proud of that, and it seemed to lift his spirits immensely. The day before his birthday, a press release was issued that said in part that Duke was hoping to spend a quiet day with his entire family, and that the hospital was baking a cake for the occasion. It added, 'Wayne is in good spirits. His condition is stable. He's taking long walks in the hall, and laughing and joking.'

Unfortunately, it wasn't true on the day of the birthday itself. Duke awoke feeling miserable—uncomfortable and in terrible pain. It was, in fact, one of his worst days. Painkillers were administered, and he slept throughout most of the afternoon and into the evening. We all remained in the adjacent room, but none of us felt like celebrating. His presents remained in the closet. The cake was put away in the refrigerator. I returned to the hotel, made an effort to eat a small salad, and cried myself to sleep.

There was little improvement in Duke's condition the next morning, but in the late afternoon, after sleeping fitfully most of the day, he awoke feeling a little better. We thought it might cheer him up, so we brought the cake to his room and we all sang 'Happy Birthday.' He tried to smile and be happy, but it was all an act. He had neither the heart nor the strength to open his birthday presents, so we sent them back to Newport—'to open when you get home,' we said.

It was obvious by now that the treatments weren't doing any good. Briefly there was some talk about sending him home, but the idea was vetoed. He needed the kind of care that was available only in a hospital.

The walks were abandoned now. But when Henry

Hathaway came in for a visit on May 28, Duke insisted on sitting in his chair for the half hour Mr Hathaway remained with him. Mr Hathaway had himself undergone cancer surgery back in 1961, and had been very encouraging to Duke during the period following Duke's lung operation. I don't know what the two men talked about that afternoon, but I know the conversation was a positive one. In fact, his visit with Duke was the longest that anyone outside the family spent with him the entire time he was in the hospital.

On May 29 the doctors added morphine to Duke's IV solution. Duke had received several morphine injections at various times during the month, but now it was a regular part of his medication. The pain was that bad. What horrible thing was going to happen next? We didn't have to wait long to find out.

The next day, he was taken down to the X-ray room for a GI series, and the blockage looked so bad the doctors decided to dilate his esophagus the next day to see if that would help. It didn't. The blockage was practically total now. At about this time, the immunotherapy was discontinued. One doctor said to me, 'I think we should just leave him alone now.'

A couple of nights later I was standing at Duke's bedside, holding his hand, when he started, and said, 'Did you see that flash of light?' I replied, 'No, Duke. But I wasn't looking in that direction. I was looking at you.'

What kind of light? The evening had been clear and cool, starry. There could have been no heat lightning or sudden electrical storm. Had Duke been hallucinating under the effect of the morphine? Or had there actually been a light that could be seen only by him? I had heard stories about people seeing lights shortly before their death, but had always dismissed them. Now, suddenly, I wasn't so sure, and I was frightened.

I didn't leave the ninth floor that night but curled up on the sofa in Duke's room and napped a bit. When it was light, I went over to Duke's bed, and, reassured that he was breathing regularly and sleeping peacefully, I rushed back to the Marquis for a shower and a change of clothes.

When I returned to the hospital, Alice Day was giving him his morning bath, and everything seemed normal. A little later, though, when we were alone, she solemnly advised me that Duke's blood pressure was starting to drop.

I felt there was no choice left to me. I had to confront Dr Longmire and ask the one question I had been forcing myself *not* to ask for weeks, the question for which I really didn't want to hear the answer. But I had to face reality. We all had to.

CHAPTER 22

I was in the sitting room with Melinda when Dr Longmire paid his regular morning call on Duke, and as he was leaving, I asked him to join us for a moment. I came directly to the point.

'Dr Longmire, how long does he have to live? How much time does he have left?'

He looked at me and replied, 'A few weeks.' Dr Longmire sounded so solemn and helpless. Melinda was standing next to me, and I remember the look of disbelief that came over her face. She was surprised that I had asked, and shocked at the reply. I think we all really knew the answer, but the subject had never been broached before.

I called Michael at the office.

'Dr Longmire says it's only a matter of weeks, a few weeks.'

'What are you telling me?'

'A few weeks—that's all.'

'Silence. Then, 'Was Dad told?'

'No, to the best of my knowledge, he was not told.'

Dr Longmire never said to me, 'He knows'; nor did I ever tell Duke, 'It's coming.' Nor did any of his family. We kept that dark secret to ourselves while trying to keep everything else light. If Duke had ever come out and asked, 'Pat, am I dying?' I don't know what I would have said. He could forgive anything but deliberate lies. For seven years we had been honest with each other. Could I have let our relationship end with a mortal lie? I don't think so, but he never put me to that test.

Now that we could no longer avoid the inevitable, Michael began putting the business in order and discreetly making plans for the funeral, using subterfuge, I'm sure, so that the press wouldn't know what was going on. The last thing Duke needed was to hear the news of his impending death from Walter Cronkite. Toni and Patrick were informed immediately. We all thought it wiser not to upset Aissa, Marisa, or Ethan, however. They should be spared the grief as long as possible.

I think Duke's closest friends may have sensed the truth, but they never discussed it. It was about this time that Arturo McGowan came for a visit and brought a Peruvian faith healer with him. I remember thinking, What *is* this? They came two or three times, when the nurse was on her dinner break, and stayed about a half hour each time. It was not something the hospital was aware of, and of course it did no good. There was too much finality to Dr Longmire's words: 'A few weeks.'

There weren't many reporters downstairs now. Duke had been hospitalized so many times in that last eighteen months that I'm sure they felt this was just another false alarm. Those who remained seemed unfamiliar. I brushed past them, unrecognized.

In spite of the medication, Duke forced himself to remain alert, but it was in and out, in and out; sleeping for short periods, waking, sleeping. We had nurses around the clock, of course, but one of us had to be there at all times to help her. Duke couldn't even sip water without its coming up. I'd help Alice Day turn him over, and change the sheets, which had to be done at regular intervals. He'd sometimes say, 'I'm sorry,' to us, but he never complained, never. He just had that weak, helpless look in his eyes.

I'd look at his wasted body with horror and shame: horror at what had happened to the man and shame that I could be horrified at the sight of the body of someone I loved so much. No one should be allowed

227

to die in that way. The horrible 'cancer odor' I had heard of—now I knew it. The room reeked of it.

I had heard the expression 'vital signs' on those television doctor shows, but I had never really bothered to think about what the term really meant. I had never thought about death or been present when anyone died. I had pictured it happening as in the movies— peaceful and smooth, time for a lingering farewell, then the heart stops and it's over.

Now we were all concerned about the 'vital signs.' And they kept deteriorating.

On June 5, I believe, I noticed that one of the IV bottles was gone, the bottle with that special preparation that had been responsible for Duke's adding nine pounds. The older children and I had a private meeting with the doctor. We were told that sometimes patients could be kept alive by trying to keep their weight up, but that in those cases they often died screaming. None of us wanted that.

It wasn't as if the cord had been unplugged on some lifesaving device, such as a heart or lung machine. The IV had been only a prolonging tactic, to be used when there was a chance of survival.

On June 6 Michael asked me to drive to Newport Beach with him—it concerned some business—and on the way it suddenly occurred to me that it was my birthday. Somehow it didn't matter. I felt as if I were dying, too. My whole world was falling apart. My life of seven years was about to end, and I couldn't picture a life without Duke.

When I got back to the hospital, Aissa handed me three or four unsigned birthday cards—all from Duke. He had been sleeping when I'd left for Newport, but when he'd awakened, he had remembered it was my birthday and asked Aissa to go down to the gift shop and buy some birthday cards so he could choose and sign one. By the time Aissa had returned from the gift shop, Duke had been sleeping again, so Aissa just handed me the cards—'from Dad'—together with a card of her own and a box of soap. She must have reminded the other kids, too, because Melinda and Greg brought me a basket with a plant and a bottle of wine in it and a little bird perched on top, and Patrick gave me a card as well. They tried to make it cheerful for me, and I was very grateful for that—to know that they cared.

I was now spending every night in the hospital, sleeping fitfully on the sofa in Duke's room in case he awakened and wanted me for something. In the morning, knowing he had passed safely through the night, I'd return to my room, shower, change clothes, have some coffee, and return.

On June 8 Duke was in and out of a semicoma throughout the day, and Alice Day told me his respiration was going down. It must have been late that night that I started packing his personal effects, so that when 'it' finally happened, the suitcases could be picked up and taken away, quietly and without confusion. I packed almost by rote, trying to block from my mind the significance of what I was doing, yet it was a horrifying thing to have to pack his belongings, and there was always the fear: What if he should wake up and see me doing this? What would I say? It was something that had to be done, though, and I did it as calmly as I could.

Calmly—until I opened the top drawer of his dresser. Suddenly I was seized by waves of nausea. Lying there—neatly folded in plastic and accompanied by all the necessary instructions—was a shroud. It was the first time in my life I had ever seen one, something I had never even thought about until that very minute. I closed the drawer quickly. I never mentioned to anyone that I had seen it. But I remembered it. I still do. There was this giant of a man in his big bed, and a few feet away, a shroud, waiting. Dr Longmire had said, 'A few weeks.' Now I knew it was merely a matter of days, possibly hours.

On Saturday, June 9, we were bracing ourselves for

it; we were certain that that would be the day. Dr Longmire had gone to his house in the San Diego area for the weekend. Throughout the day, all of Duke's vital signs progressively got weaker. Finally Alice Day phoned Dr Longmire and advised him to return to UCLA Medical Center immediately, which he did.

Duke was in a semicoma, unconscious all day. We didn't think he would come out of this one. He was oblivious to our voices, to everything. But then, suddenly, at nine P.M., he woke up, and remained awake and alert for three hours. He was laughing, kidding around, sounding like the man he had been before his illness. He wanted to watch some television. All the children were there. None of us could believe what we were seeing and hearing.

He appeared quite lucid, and he knew where he was, but from the gist of his conversation I think he thought he was still working, still making movies and appearing on television. He kept talking a great deal about CBS that night, and making jokes about it. I don't know why, and I can't remember the jokes, just that we were an appreciative audience—appreciative that he was awake, and appreciative that he actually seemed happy. His blue eyes were shining. He showed no pain. He seemed to be enjoying every moment of those three hours, that one final burst of life.

We didn't fool ourselves that a miracle had occurred, that he had passed another crisis and would be all right again. We all knew he couldn't live much longer, but it was so wonderful to see him awake and talking, able to recognize us and to leave us with something positive to remember.

Shortly before midnight he fell asleep again, and I spent the night on the sofa in his room, worried that he might die and that I wouldn't be there with him and that he would know I wasn't. I wanted to be with Duke when it happened. I didn't want him to be alone or with a nurse.

The following morning, I helped the nurse change

his sheets and raced back to my hotel for an hour, then back to the hospital. Duke slept through the day and night, without interruption. Mainly I just sat there, looking at him. His personal effects had all been sent back home, with no one the wiser. Everything was in order. The drawers were all empty—all but that one top drawer.

I remember being terrified that the end would come when I'd gone downstairs for a cup of coffee or down the hall for a cigarette, or even to the next room to take care of the telephone calls.

On the morning of June 11 Duke was in a semicoma again, but breathing. I was waiting for Alice Day, who had the seven-to-three shift, to arrive before returning to the Marquis to freshen up. I remember standing at Duke's bedside, looking at him and talking to him, even though I knew he couldn't hear me. Suddenly he opened his eyes and stared up at me blankly for a few minutes.

'Duke,' I said. 'Do you know me? Do you know who I am?'

And he replied, 'Of course I know who you are. You're my girl. I love you.'

Those were the last words I heard Duke say. Then he closed his eyes and went back into a deep coma. When Alice Day came on duty, she must have known instinctively that he would not come out of it, because once Patrick and Aissa had arrived at the hospital, Alice volunteered to stay through the night shift if we'd like her to do so. That was the only time since Duke's hospitalization that she had made such an offer.

Of course, we wanted her to stay. The other nurses were capable and efficent, but Alice and been with us at Newport and we regarded her as more than just another nurse.

Patrick, Marisa, Aissa, Toni, Melinda, Ethan, and I spent most of the day in the sitting room. Michael was at his office. Alice came in periodically to tell us about Duke's vital signs. It was an endless afternoon. Then Alice signaled us to come into Duke's room.

He was still alive—we could see him breathing, hear him breathing—but it was evident that there was a lengthier passage of time between each breath. A gasp, then silence: another gasp, a longer period of silence. Then, just as we thought it was over, yet another gasp. Then, finally the room became eerily still, and remained so. It was exactly five-twenty-three P.M., Pacific Daylight Time.

I recall that Patrick said, 'Bye, Dad.' I leaned over and kissed his forehead and whispered, 'Bye, Duke. I love you.'

We all just stood there for a few minutes, all with our own private thoughts.

Then I turned to Patrick and said, 'We have to call.'

Michael had given us instructions about whom to call so that Duke could be removed from the hospital without any outsiders knowing. It had been so carefully planned.

We looked at Duke one final time, and as Alice Day moved towards the dresser and began opening the top drawer, we went into an adjoining room.

Patrick made the necessary phone call. He also called Michael, I believe. The girls and I sat there in a daze, sobbing. No one was hysterical.

As we headed for the elevator, someone greeted us with a cheery, 'Hi, how are you today?' I replied, 'Fine, how are you?' as if nothing had happened. We couldn't allow anyone to know.

The girls and I returned to the Westwood Marquis. They went directly to their room; I returned to mine, to get my things together.

The phone rang. It was Michael. He wanted to know if I'd be able to drive to Newport by myself. I told him yes, I'd be fine.

By the time I got to the desk, the Waynes had already checked out. I told the person at the desk that Duke was doing better and we had decided to return

232

to Newport for a few days; then I made reservations for Marisa and myself for the following Tuesday, so no one would suspect anything had happened.

The drive back to Newport by myself was a good one for me. It helped me to get my thoughts together, and I had to concentrate on the road. I remember turning on the radio and hearing traffic reports, baseball scores, weather. No special bulletins.

Rosa heard my footsteps on the walkway of the side entrance to the house. When she saw my face she knew immediately and started to cry.

I went inside the house and turned on the radio again. The dial had been set to an all-music station, and when I turned it on, the theme from *The High and the Mighty* resounded throughout Duke's den. Until that moment, I had had a tight rein on my emotions, but now I just slumped in Duke's favorite chair, his private chair, and let it all pour out as the station's tribute to Duke continued. It was nearly eight o'clock. The news was out. The phone began ringing incessantly. I fought to regain my composure.

My life with Duke had come to an end two and a half hours earlier, but I was still on Batjac's payroll, still 'the late John Wayne's secretary.' There was a great deal of work left to be done, a great many secrets to be guarded. There was no time for personal grief. That would come later.

CHAPTER 23

ONLY Duke's family and I knew where Duke's body had been moved to. We were determined not to have his death turn into a sideshow.

Michael had chosen the Laguna Hills Mortuary and had sworn Joseph O'Connor, the mortician, to secrecy. The address of Duke's house had often been publicized, though, and shortly after the death announcement on the television, dozens of cars began invading Bayshore Drive—the morbid, the curious, and those who just wanted to pay their last respects and knew no other way. The traffic became so intense that I had to phone for private security guards to keep out intruders, a measure Duke had always scoffed at, even though he had been away from home so much. Even in spite of the security, a young man was discovered asleep the next morning in the alcove between the wrought-iron double doors and the main door that led to the house.

I called in a locksmith and had all the locks changed, as yet another precautionary measure. Rosa and the executors were given all the keys. I kept the key to the office door.

That morning, Duke's death made headlines all over the world, but I was not interested in looking at the papers. I knew that Duke's obituary had been planned for some time, with only the day and time to be filled in, along with comments from Duke's friends. Said Bob Hope: 'He was a big, big chunk of America. Wayne meant a lot to America. He loved to promote America. He stood for America. I don't think he saw himself as a symbol. He just wanted to do the things he wanted to do, and those were right for America.'

From President Carter: 'He was bigger than life. In an age of few heroes, he was the genuine article. But he was more than a hero; he was a symbol of many of the qualities that made America great. The ruggedness, the rough independence, the sense of personal courage, on and off the screen, reflected the best of our national character.' And so on.

My man was dead. Long live the legend.

We had lowered the flag outside Duke's patio to half mast. That was a personal gesture, but then the Los Angeles County Board of Supervisors ordered the flags on all county buildings flown at half mast. Subsequently a resolution was introduced to change the name of the Orange County Airport to the John Wayne Airport. It was passed on June 20. The Olympic torch atop the Los Angeles Coliseum was lighted, to burn until after Duke's funeral.

Meanwhile we who had loved him were making plans for the funeral, taking precautions so that no one would know the exact time or even the date. Even when I phoned my friend Peggy in Louisiana and asked her to fly in as soon as possible and to stay with me until after the funeral, I was vague about the date.

On June 12 Michael phoned to ask me to go across the road and select the clothes in which Duke would be buried. I forgot to ask whether I should send shorts and shoes and socks, too, and I remember feeling stupid about that. I had had no experience with that kind of thing. Rosa let me in, and followed me into Duke's dressing room, unable to stop crying as I went through his closets.

I chose a new black suit he had ordered at the same time he had his tuxedo made for the Academy Awards, just two months earlier. I also picked out a beige shirt with a button-down collar, a maroon tie, black shoes and socks, white shorts—and for some reason I added a blue scarf to be placed in the pocket of Duke's suit. The mortician's wife came by to pick

235

up the clothing. I remember wondering who was going to dress him, and how anyone would want such a job. I also remember that during the last two years of his life, Duke occasionally expressed a preference for cremation, with his ashes to be strewn from the *Wild Goose* off Catalina Island. But he always added, 'The kids would be horrified,' so he had made no such request in his will.

On June 13 Michael called and asked me to drive to the mortuary, where he and Melinda would meet me. There Michael took me into a room filled with different models of coffins and asked my opinion. I didn't care for any of them, and obviously Michael didn't, either, because he later drove to Los Angeles to look at others. The funeral director asked if Melinda and I wanted to see the body again. Melinda and I both said no.

The family had requested that no flowers be sent, either from the public or from friends, but Melinda and I were deputized to arrange for the family flowers: anthuriums to cover the coffin. Duke had had a regular florist, but because we still didn't want anyone to know about the funeral plans, we decided to go to a florist where we weren't known. As we were placing the order, the saleslady naturally asked, 'And what is the name of the deceased?' Without skipping a beat, Melinda replied, 'Greg Muñoz,' her husband's name. It was like something out of a black comedy. Here, at the saddest point of our lives, we had to stop ourselves from breaking out in laughter at the thought that the woman might call Melinda's house and Greg would answer. The florist made a point of telling us how expensive the anthuriums would be. 'Money is no object,' I replied.

On June 14 Archbishop McGrath came by to comfort me. As ill as he was, Milton Bren also drove down to make sure I was all right, since Claire had gone to New York for a couple of days. I couldn't eat anything, I had no interest in food. The day of the funeral was finally set for the next day, June 15, at Our Lady Queen of Angels parish, a very simple, modern church in the Newport Beach area. Archbishop McGrath would conduct Mass at five-forty-five A.M., when most of the town would be asleep. In addition to the family, myself, and Rosa, only a very few close friends attended the service: the Johnsons from Arizona, Chick Iverson, Arturo McGowan. Joe DeFranco was in Europe at the time. None of Duke's movie friends, no politicians, and certainly no press were invited. Somehow, though a photographer found out where we were, because a photograph was taken as we were leaving the service and was sent out over the wires that day. Other than that, we were not disturbed. Later we drove to Pacific View Memorial Park, where, in a plot of land overlooking Newport Bay, Duke's body was put to rest.

Duke had always said that when he died, he hoped that afterward everyone would go out and have a drink and try not to be sad. So after the burial everyone gathered for a breakfast and reception at Pilar Wayne's house nearby. Then we all went our separate ways.

It was over.

Later that night, I decided to return to Pacific View. I wanted to be alone with Duke one last time—at the 'mystic hour,' which, as we were approaching the longest day of the year, now fell at about eight-thirty. The park officially closed at five P.M., but my name was on the list to be admitted, so they allowed me in.

The blanket of anthuriums had been moved. Later I learned that to avoid problems, a second, fresh grave had been dug nearby and the flowers had been placed there, so that Duke's resting place would not be disturbed by either souvenir hunters or vandals. Fans who came bringing flowers were asked to place them at the foot of the flagpole by the entrance.

I took one anthurium that night—and pressed it. I still have it.

EPILOGUE

ON June 19 Duke's attorney, John S. Warren, filed Duke's twenty-seven-page last will and testament in Orange County Superior Court. The following morning the local papers headlined JOHN WAYNE WILL—$6.8 MILLION—MOSTLY TO CHILDREN. It sounded enormous.

One had to read the story very carefully to realize that most of that sum represented property and other holdings and only a very small portion was in cash. The newspapers made much of the fact that Pilar, Duke's legal widow, was not included in the will, but she had been provided for in the separation agreement. All of the children were taken care of in the will, as was Duke's first wife, Josephine, and, to a lesser extent, as were Mary St John and I.

Michael was kind. He told me not to worry. I could stay in my little house until the lease was up, and I would be kept on the Batjac payroll for the rest of the year, or until I found other employment, whichever came first.

Throughout most of July I worked in my little office in Duke's house, clearing up paperwork. I would have to leave before the 'mystic hour' came, though. I couldn't stand to be there when dusk fell on Newport Bay.

Milton and Claire Bren were marvelous and understanding beyond belief, considering their own problems. Claire called as soon as she returned from New York and said, 'Don't argue. Get into your car and come over to cocktails and dinner.' I did. That invitation was repeated many times over. Maureen O'Hara called frequently from the Virgin Islands. Even though she was thousands of miles away, I felt as though she were there with me. Those two women had been so important in Duke's life, and now they cared about what was going to happen to me now that Duke was gone.

Many of the other people Duke and I had known sent letters, sharing their sense of loss with me. The loveliest was from Katharine Hepburn. She wrote:

Phyllis [her secretary] and I have talked about you and thought of you, and while John was alive were so happy for him that he had you right there helping him down the last path. I hope he got my few notes. It is so hard to say what one really wants to say. You were so sweet to him on the picture. And seemed to have such a good sense of what was common sense. And you fixed it so that he could survive what must have been a long agony. He seemed so like Spencer to me. I felt that I had known him forever and I am sure you must feel wildly sad. But at least you know that you did a good job and one that only you could do . . .

One of the things that helped me get through Duke's death was the fact that I did feel I had done everything I could do. Nevertheless, the feeling of loneliness was almost unbearable at times. The DeFrancos were very supportive. They, too, invited me to dinner frequently, although I was hardly a cheerful guest. I went through sieges of self-pity. I recall standing on Joe's patio, crying, saying, 'What am I going to do? What's going to become of me now that Duke's gone?' I felt so scared, so lost. Joe and Barbara tried to comfort me. They told me that everything would work out, that Duke had told him, 'Pat will be all right. She'll get on with it.'

In October the wife of a friend of Duke's and I flew to London for a vacation, but I still couldn't give up

Duke's ghost. I returned to all the places Duke and I had been to together: the Athenaeum Hotel, the White Elephant. I relived it all. I knew it wasn't healthy, but I couldn't stop myself. I couldn't let go.

When I returned to California, however, I knew I *had* to do something. I had to find a new place to live and a new job, and to get away from Newport Beach. I finally rented a charming apartment in Marina Del Rey. Finding a job wasn't as easy, but once again Claire came to my rescue. Her stepson, Donald Bren, was looking for an executive secretary for his real-estate firm. She invited us both to dinner one night. We talked. I was hired and went to work for the Bren Company in November.

It wasn't a very merry Christmas. Even now, that is when it hurts the most—at Christmas—without Duke. It *was* the dawn of a bright new decade, however, and I, who had never believed in New Year's resolutions, resolved to block the memories of my years with Duke from my mind, resolved to 'let go.' It was foolish of me to think I could.

I took all of my photo albums and Duke's cards, my diaries and the souvenirs of our trips together, and put them in storage. But you can't lock away memories, not when there are reminders everywhere. A week seldom passes when one of Duke's films isn't shown on television, or when some columnist or politician or business leader refers to the 'John Wayne spirit.' John Wayne posters and key rings and dolls are everywhere.

When I started to work on this story, I felt compelled to return to Newport Beach, to see Duke's house again and board the *Wild Goose* once more. The ship is berthed in San Pedro harbor now, and its new owner, Lynn Hutchins, invited me aboard. It was almost as Duke had left it. The brass railings were spit-and-polish bright, the plaques all in place. The chairs and benches had been reupholstered, but in the same leather as before. There were a great many photos of Duke on the walls. Mr Hutchins even claimed he sometimes

240

thought he heard Duke's footsteps walking the deck at night, when everything was still.

Duke's house on Bayshore Drive has been sold to an elderly millionairess. For a few minutes, standing in front of it, I became lost in the past. There were so many memories—of the people who had been there, the good times, the children's laughter, of Duke and me calling it a day and strolling out to the patio for the 'mystic hour.'

But, of course, it wasn't the same. The house was unfurnished when I saw it and in the process of being remodeled. A façade had been built over the entrance, to create the illusion of a two-storey house, and a skylight was being chipped out of the ceiling in the den. On the patio, Duke's favorite wrought-iron bench was turned over on its side, unpainted and rusting.

I burst into tears. How dare they do this to Duke's house. I thought. But of course it was no longer Duke's house. Even if no changes had been made, the house would still have been a shell. It was the man who had made the house come alive.

Before I left for home, I drove to the Pacific View Memorial Park. I hadn't been to Duke's grave for many months. It was still unmarked. Duke had wanted a simple epitaph—'Feo, Fuerte y Formal' (Ugly, Strong, and with Dignity)—on a small plaque with his name, but only a patch of grass covered his lonely grave. And still does. How ironic that his name is everywhere, but not on his final resting place.

There is a poem that Duke read as a eulogy at Howard Hawks's funeral:

> *Do not stand at my grave and weep:*
> *I am not there, I do not sleep.*
> *I am a thousand winds that blow.*
> *I am the diamond glint on snow.*
> *I am the sunlight on ripened grain.*
> *I am the gentle autumn rain.*
> *When you awaken in the morning's hush,*

241

I am the swift uplifting rush
Of quiet birds in the circled flight,
I am the soft stars that shine at night.
Do not stand at my grave and cry;
I am not there, I did not die.

He did not die. As I stood there at his grave, I felt him with me. Duke had such a marvelous mixture of qualities I loved: innocence, directness, simplicity, a childlike sense of wonder. He had such a wonderful way of giving himself completely to the moment. When he was with me, he was completely with me, as if we were on an island frozen in time.

I have put my life in order, but some part of me will always be on that island with him. With Duke. The man I loved, not the legend.